MW00475107

Praise for
Challenging Learning Through Feedback
by James Nottingham and Jill Nottingham

With the rapid emergence of formative assessment used in support of learning, refinements also are emerging in our understanding of how to use of descriptive feedback during learning to promote student success. This new book provides the most up-to-date and complete treatment synthesis of those understandings. Rare is the book that offers guidance both to scholars and practitioners, but this book does both.

—Rick Stiggins
Assessment Consultant
Corwin Author

James Nottingham's work on Challenging Learning is a critical element of creating Visible Learners. This new series will help teachers hone the necessary pedagogical skills of dialogue, feedback, questioning and mindset. There's no better resource to encourage all learners to know and maximize their impact!

—John Hattie
Professor and Director
Melbourne Education Research Institute
University of Melbourne, Australia

This book is a must-have for teachers. It's easy to read and easy to implement. Feedback provided at the right time and in the right manner increases student motivation and learning outcome. It is relevant for all grade levels.

—Joyce Sager
Reading Teacher for Dyslexic High School Students
Gadsden, AL

Feedback—a noun or a verb? A separate practice or an integral part of the learning process? Something we do "to students" or "with students"? The Nottinghams sort it all out for us—the "what," "why" and "how" of the process and the practice of feedback. A simply and elegantly organized book with tons of resources that guide educators to practice quality feedback. A must-read for all teacher teams!

—Barb Pitchford
Co-Author, Leading Impact Teams: Building a Culture of Efficacy

This was a thought-provoking read and one I will reference over and over again. The authors have created a thorough reference for all teachers working to make their feedback impact learning, not only student learning, but their own. This will be a valuable reference for educators for years to come. I think that this reaches beyond classroom walls and will also help administrators model feedback for teachers and make an impact on the growth of student achievement.

—Katina Keener
Elementary Principal
Hayes, VA

This is a timely, well-researched, practical view into the teachers' view of Visible Learning and all this research can do to advance learning for all students. Written in an engaging, example-filled, light, humorous style, it gives the reader some real, practical examples of formative assessment strategies, clarity about learning intentions and success criteria, the essence of good lesson design. It's what we have been waiting for to make Visible Learning come alive for our teachers in the classroom.

—Ainsley B. Rose
Corwin Consultant
West Kelowna, BC, Canada

A great tool for professional development and personal growth for any educator. This book is the add-on I need during feedback sessions. Teachers need the examples and explanations this book offers.

—**Harry Dickens**
Education Consultant, Texarkana, TX

This book is for anyone who wants to help others get better. I found myself taking notes in chapter after chapter because of the practical advice based on succinct summaries of research and evidence. I could incorporate the ideas in my classes the next day. Nottingham and Nottingham remind us that "to assess" means "to sit beside." They come alongside us as readers to help us better understand how to move beyond advice and evaluation to feedback that leads to improvement.

—**Jon Eckert**
Associate Professor, Wheaton College
Author, The Novice Advantage
Wheaton, IL

This book is an accessible and comprehensive guide—one that provides the whole picture when it comes to offering quality feedback to deepen student learning. Each chapter ends with questions that inspired me to reflect and take a hard look at where I am in my feedback journey. Busy instructional leaders will appreciate the organizational structure of the book as well as the clear definitions and practical examples that can be used to help teachers envision the ideas into practice.

—**Abbey S. Duggins**
Assistant Principal for Instruction, Saluda High School
Author, Using Quality Feedback to Guide Professional Learning
Saluda, SC

Finally, a practical book on feedback for teachers! The Nottinghams cut through the hype and misinformation and bring teachers a valuable tool they will want to revisit often throughout their career. It is written with the teacher in mind, lesson plan in hand, and relevant to all in education. The perfect schoolwide book-study book!

—**Lisa Cebelak**
Education Consultant, Grand Rapids, MI

James and Jill Nottingham have once again equipped educators with practical applications and examples of how not only to increase learning, but also ensure it will happen at the greatest possible levels. They provide teachers with strategies for creating the culture their classrooms need to help students reach the "Eureka moments" where learning becomes accelerated by the students . . . and their desire to grow and learn even more is augmented. Finally, they deliver rich guiding examples for teachers to increase teacher clarity through the development of high-quality learning intentions and success criteria to help students know when they have met these intentions. This is an essential foundational element for feedback to have a place to originate from and be effective for learning. I highly recommend this book as a bucket-list read for any educator!

—**Dave Nagel**
Education Consultant
Author, Effective Grading Practices for Secondary Teachers
Indianapolis, IN

Not only does this book support teachers in developing a deep understanding of quality descriptive feedback, but the authors also give practical examples of how to design learning intentions and success criteria to lift the quality of feedback during lessons. The authors offer innovative feedback tools based on *The Learning Challenge*; these innovative tools will support teachers in ensuring that feedback is reliable and valid when partnering with students to create a true learning culture!

—**Paul Bloomberg**
Education Consultant, The Core Collaborative
Co-Author, Leading Impact Teams: Building a Culture of Efficacy
San Diego, CA

CHALLENGING
LEARNING Through
FEEDBACK

Challenging Learning Series

The Learning Challenge: How to Guide Your Students Through the Learning Pit to Achieve Deeper Understanding

by James Nottingham

Challenging Learning Through Dialogue

by James Nottingham, Jill Nottingham and Martin Renton

Challenging Learning Through Feedback

by James Nottingham and Jill Nottingham

Challenging Learning Through Mindset

by James Nottingham and Bosse Larsson

Challenging Learning Through Questioning

by James Nottingham and Martin Renton

Learning Challenge Lessons, Elementary

by James Nottingham, Jill Nottingham, Lucy Thompson and Mark Bollom

Learning Challenge Lessons, Secondary ELA

by James Nottingham, Jill Nottingham, Lucy Thompson and Mark Bollom

Learning Challenge Lessons, Secondary Mathematics

by James Nottingham, Jill Nottingham, Lucy Thompson and Mark Bollom

Learning Challenge Lessons, Secondary Science/STEM

by James Nottingham, Jill Nottingham, Lucy Thompson and Mark Bollom

James Nottingham ■ Jill Nottingham

Foreword by Larry Ainsworth

CHALLENGING LEARNING Through FEEDBACK

How to Get the Type, Tone and Quality
of Feedback Right Every Time

CORWIN
A SAGE Publishing Company

FOR INFORMATION

Corwin

A SAGE Company

2455 Teller Road

Thousand Oaks, California 91320

(800) 233-9936

www.corwin.com

SAGE Publications Ltd.

1 Oliver's Yard

55 City Road

London, EC1Y 1SP

United Kingdom

SAGE Publications India Pvt. Ltd.

B 1/I 1 Mohan Cooperative Industrial Area

Mathura Road, New Delhi 110 044

India

SAGE Publications Asia-Pacific Pte. Ltd.

3 Church Street

#10-04 Samsung Hub

Singapore 049483

Acquisitions Editor: Ariel Bartlett

Senior Associate Editor: Desirée A. Bartlett

Editorial Assistant: Kaitlyn Irwin

Production Editors: Cassandra Margaret Seibel
    and Melanie Birdsall

Copy Editor: Sarah J. Duffy

Typesetter: Hurix Systems Pvt. Ltd.

Proofreader: Caryne Brown

Indexer: Diggs Publication Services

Cover Designer: Janet Kiesel

Marketing Manager: Jill Margulies

Printed in the United States of America.

Library of Congress Cataloging-in-Publication Data

Names: Nottingham, James, author. | Nottingham, Jill, author.

Title: Challenging learning through feedback : how to get the type, tone and quality of feedback right every time / by James Nottingham and Jill Nottingham.

Description: Thousand Oaks, California : Corwin, a SAGE company, [2017] | Series: Challenging learning series | Includes bibliographical references and index.

Identifiers: LCCN 2016044631 | ISBN 9781506376479 (pbk. : alk. paper)

Subjects: LCSH: Teaching—Methodology. | Communication in education. | Teacher-student relationships.

Classification: LCC LB1025.3 .N677 2017b | DDC 371.102—dc23 LC record available at https://lccn.loc.gov/2016044631

US Edition

This book is printed on acid-free paper.

17 18 19 20 21 10 9 8 7 6 5 4 3 2 1

CONTENTS

Chapter 7: Seven Steps to Feedback   121

Chapter 8: Tools for Feedback   135

Repertoire and Judgment Notes   149

References   157

Index   160

LIST OF FIGURES

THE CHALLENGING LEARNING STORY

Challenging Learning was the title I used for my first book back in 2010. I chose the title because it brought together two key themes of my work and it gave a relevant double meaning—challenging the way in which learning takes place and showing how to make learning more challenging.

More recently, Challenging Learning is the name I've given to a group of organizations set up in seven countries. These educational companies bring together some of the very best teachers and leaders I know. Together we transform the most up-to-date and impressive research into best pedagogical practices for schools, preschools and colleges.

This book continues in the same tradition: challenging learning and making learning more challenging. The main difference between this book and the original *Challenging Learning* title is that this one focuses on practical resources for use by teachers, support staff and leaders. There is still some theory, but now the emphasis is on pedagogical tools and strategies. Across this new series you will find books about questions and the zone of proximal development, feedback and progress, mindset and self-efficacy, coaching for professional development and leadership and organization.

This particular volume focuses on feedback and its role in helping students make progress. Here my co-authors and I share some of the best ways to ensure feedback is powerful and productive. We show how feedback can be improved by changing the timing of it. We also show you how to engage your students in giving feedback to themselves and each other. And we show you just how important success criteria can be in helping students answer the three central feedback questions: What am I trying to achieve? How much progress have I made so far? What should I do next?

I am delighted to say I have written this book in collaboration with Jill Nottingham and our team at Challenging Learning. Together we have blended the best of what we have all been working on for the last twenty years or more.

For the sake of clarity, the term *we* is used to represent ideas from Jill and me. Individual stories are prefaced with our first names. Where an idea or strategy comes from one of the other authors, then we have prefaced that section with their full names, for example, Martin Renton or Gordon Poad.

As you read this book, you will notice that we refer mainly to *teachers* and *teaching*. Please do not take this to mean this book is only for teachers. In fact, the book is aimed at support staff and leaders as much as at teachers. We simply use the terms *teacher* and *teaching* as shorthand for the position and pedagogy of all the professions working in schools.

Most chapters begin with a preview. This is to give you a chance to think about your current practice before diving in to see what our recommendations are. Chatting with a colleague about what you think works well (and how you know it does); what you would like to change; and, in an ideal world, what you would like your pedagogy to be like will definitely help you use this book as the reflective journal it is intended to be.

At the end of each chapter, we include a review. This is focused on repertoire and judgment. A broad repertoire—or tool kit of teaching strategies, as some authors call it— is crucial to improving pedagogy. Yet repertoire alone is not sufficient; good judgment is also needed. So, whereas the strategies in this book should be sufficient to broaden your repertoire, your good judgment will come from reflections on your own experiences, from trying out the new strategies with your students and from dialogue with your colleagues. Our suggestions for review are there to help you with your reflections.

Finally, the Next Steps section of each chapter is included to emphasize how much your actions count. As a teacher, teaching assistant or leader, you are among the most powerful influences on student learning. Back when you were a secondary student and went from teacher to teacher, you knew exactly which members of staff had high expectations and which had low, which had a good sense of humor and which you suspected had not laughed since childhood. It is the same today. Your students know what your expectations and ethos are. So it is not the government, students' parents or the curriculum that sets the culture (though they all have influence). It is you who sets the culture, and so it is your actions that count most.

With this book I hope we can inspire you to ever more expert actions.

With best wishes,

James Nottingham

FOREWORD

"Feedback is complex. That's why this book has been written: to help find a way through the maze!"

This quote from *Challenging Learning Through Feedback* captures the essential message and focus of co-authors James Nottingham and Jill Nottingham—to demystify what feedback *is* and to show, through numerous illustrative examples, how to use it most effectively to improve student learning.

Let's start with their comprehensive definition of feedback: "information we receive that helps to *shape our next response*. It can be formal or informal. Feedback provokes a response. Feedback is information with which a student can confirm, add to, overwrite or fine-tune their thoughts and/or actions."

They posit three first-person questions that should "drive all feedback" relative to a *student's* learning needs:

1. What am I trying to achieve?

2. How much progress have I made so far?

3. What should I do next?

The authors explain, "Feedback should help students close the gap between where they are now and where they want to be next. Feedback should help students understand the goal or learning intention, know where they are in relation to the goal and realize what they need to bridge the gap."

A powerful reading moment for me was their persuasive position that feedback can be dramatically improved simply by changing the timing of it. Feedback should come *after* a student's first attempts at a task but *before* that task is completed.

Effective feedback must be offered *in relation to criteria* that identify what a successful learning outcome should look like. Success criteria—the specifics of what students are to do to demonstrate their attainment of the learning intention—are essential to communicating expectations clearly, especially when coupled with worked examples matched to the success criteria.

In 2008, Dr. John Hattie wrote, "The effect of feedback on learning . . . suggests average percentiles on learning outcomes of between 50% and 83% improvement." More recently, Dr. Hattie has identified the effect size of *well-implemented* feedback at 0.75, representing nearly two years of student growth in one year's time. The consummate benefit of this book is its thorough presentation of practical and doable ways busy classroom teachers can implement feedback *well*.

Here are a few of the informational gems from selected chapters that I found particularly noteworthy.

Chapter 1 includes an excellent feedback checklist listing specific criteria that all feedback should ideally meet. Two criteria I found particularly significant:

- "The quality of feedback should be judged not on what is given but by the *effect* it has on improving student performance and understanding."

- Feedback should emphasize that "*effort* leads to increased learning and that mistakes are an important part of the learning process," pointing out that praise should be directed to the *effort* students make, not to the students themselves.

Chapter 2 stresses the importance of feedback being *ongoing*, and not a one-shot event. It needs to be "timed just right: not too soon (as this will prevent students learning) and not too late (as this will reduce the chance of students making use of the feedback)." Feedback given too late causes the students to lose interest and breaks the flow of learning.

Chapter 3 describes how to create a culture of feedback, in which all students welcome feedback—*if* they believe it will help them make progress. The critical component for creating a culture of feedback is for teachers to continually convey this message: making mistakes is a regular part of any learning process, and no one should feel ashamed or bashful about making mistakes.

Chapter 4 establishes the need for clearly identifying and articulating learning goals *before* attempting to provide students with meaningful feedback. The chapter showcases the many benefits of effective learning intentions and success criteria and explains how to involve students in co-creating them.

Chapter 5 focus on taxonomies to support goal setting. Taxonomies show the steps that must be taken to succeed at a given task, from simple to complex. They can be used to "generate the right feedback at the right time for the right student." The authors present three different taxonomies, noting their respective usefulness in developing learning intentions and success criteria and in generating high-quality feedback. "Taxonomies should be used to inspire, challenge and identify the next steps in learning."

Chapter 6 presents feedback with specific reference to the SOLO (Structure of Observed Learning Outcomes) taxonomy, originated by John Biggs and Kevin Collis. Not yet as well known in the United States as other taxonomies for learning but prominent in the United Kingdom, Canada, Australia and New Zealand, SOLO is an extremely useful means for describing the different phases and stages of learning, progressing from no knowledge to deep understanding. Here, SOLO is presented as a very student-friendly framework that helps students understand where they are in the learning process. It is a valuable tool that teachers use when matching learning experiences and feedback to their students' current level of understanding.

The authors refer to Chapter 7, which presents the Seven Steps to Feedback, as the most important chapter in the book because it shows exactly *how* to make feedback work wonderfully without adding to a teacher's workload: "The Seven Steps is not about working harder, it is about working smarter! It is about teaching your students how to give themselves and each other brilliant feedback so that you become less and less needed, rather than more and more busy."

Thinking back to my own former classroom teaching experience of twenty-four years, I especially liked the sequence presented in which students are self- and peer-assessing their initial work products *first*, then editing on their own—*before* asking for and receiving teacher feedback. This depends on creating that classroom culture of feedback so that students view feedback as information that can be used to make progress. When that is established, the best kind of feedback is "advice and suggestions" related to the learning intentions and success criteria.

To work smarter and not harder, "give lots and lots of verbal feedback and reduce the amount of written feedback. Remember that the Seven Steps still involve only one round of feedback from you, so in many ways you won't be giving any more feedback than you have been doing so far. . . . Reduce the number of times you give feedback, but *increase the quality.* Even with less feedback your students will still be making more progress. Everyone's a winner!"

With this book as your guide, you now have the means to turn this vision of what effective feedback can achieve into a reality in your own classroom.

> —**Larry Ainsworth,** *Author of* Common Formative Assessments 2.0: How Teacher Teams Intentionally Align Standards, Instruction, and Assessment

ACKNOWLEDGMENTS

Corwin gratefully acknowledges the following reviewers for their editorial insight and guidance:

Harry Dickens
Education Consultant
CompassLearning
Texarkana, TX

Katina Keener
Elementary Principal
Achilles Elementary School
Hayes, VA

Ainsley B. Rose
Corwin Consultant
Visible Learning & Instructional Coaching
West Kelowna, BC, Canada

Joyce Sager
Reading Teacher for Dyslexic High School Students
Gadsden City High School
Gadsden, AL

ABOUT THE AUTHORS

James Nottingham is the founder of Challenging Learning, a company based in the United Kingdom, Australia and Scandinavia. His passion is in transforming the most up-to-date research into strategies that really work in the classroom. He has been described by the Swedish Teaching Union as "one of the most talked about names in the world of school development."

Before training to be a teacher, James worked on a pig farm, in the chemical industry, for the American Red Cross and as a sports coach in a school for deaf children. At university, he gained a first-class honors degree in education. He then worked as a teacher and leader in primary and secondary schools in the United Kingdom before co-founding an award-winning, multimillion-pound social regeneration project supporting schools and businesses across the United Kingdom.

In 2009, James was listed among the Future 500—a "definitive list of the UK's most forward-thinking and brightest innovators."

Jill Nottingham's background is in teaching, leadership and consultancy. She has been a teacher and leader in kindergartens and schools in some of the more socially deprived areas of North East England. During that time, she developed many approaches to teaching children how to learn that are still being used in schools and taught in universities today.

Jill has also trained with Edward de Bono at the University of Malta and has studied for a master's degree in education with the University of Newcastle.

Jill now leads Challenging Learning's preschool and primary school consultancy. She has written many of the Challenging Learning teaching materials, has edited the others and is currently writing three books for schools and two books for preschools. In addition to this she finds time to be the mother of three gorgeous children!

CONTRIBUTORS

James Nottingham and Jill Nottingham have written this book with contributions from the following:

- Mark Bollom
- Louise Brown
- Jill Harland
- Dan Henderson
- Gordon Poad
- Martin Renton
- Helen Richards
- Lesley Roberts
- Phil Thompson
- Sarah Unwin
- Steve Williams

All authors and all contributors can be contacted through www.challenginglearning.com.

For Ava, Harry and Phoebe
Our Children, Our World

INTRODUCTION

Feedback works. And it works brilliantly. Or so researchers tell us repeatedly. And yet it's not as simple as that because often feedback has a minimal effect—and sometimes even a negative effect. In this book, we show you how to avoid those pitfalls. We give you insight into the research evidence about what works, what doesn't and why students' own assessment capabilities are often more powerful than other forms of feedback.

We show you some of the best strategies for helping students ask the three feedback questions:

1. **What am I trying to achieve?**

2. **How much progress have I made so far?**

3. **What should I do next?**

We also show you how to make assessment, feedback and marking policies really work for all staff and students. And we help you get the timing, tone, quantity and quality of feedback right every time.

Other key points include the following:

1. The quality of feedback should be judged not on what is transmitted but on what is received and applied. (See Section 7.2.)

2. Feedback can be one of the most powerful effects on learning *if* it is timed well and used constructively. (See Chapter 7.)

3. Though feedback to students is powerful, feedback to staff is more powerful, and feedback from students to themselves is even more powerful. (See Step 3 of the Seven Steps to Feedback in Section 7.1.)

4. Grading is one of the weakest forms of feedback because it rarely helps students answer the three key feedback questions. (See Section 1.6.)

5. Feedback should be timely: coming *after* draft one (or attempt one) but *before* task completion. (See Steps 3 and 5 of the Seven Steps to Feedback in Section 7.1.)

6. Too many teachers feel the pressure to write feedback so as to impress parents or school leaders. However, feedback tends to be more powerful when it is part of a learning dialogue. (See Sections 1.2 and 7.2.)

7. Feedback from students to their teacher is absolutely necessary for personalizing learning. (See Section 2.3.7.)

> Three questions should drive feedback:
>
> What am I trying to achieve?
>
> How much progress have I made so far?
>
> What should I do next?

> The quality of feedback should be judged not on what is transmitted but on what is received and applied.

> Grading rarely helps with the feedback process because it does not answer the third feedback question (what should I do next?).

THE LANGUAGE OF LEARNING

Here are definitions for the way in which we use key terms in the book.

Assessment: the appraisal of students' work. The word has its roots in the Latin verb *assidere* meaning "to sit beside."

AfL: Assessment for Learning, used to distinguish between assessment to help with further learning and assessment *of* prior learning. It is often seen as synonymous with formative feedback (as opposed to summative feedback).

Attitudes: a tendency or preference for something. In the case of learning, we would try to encourage the attitudes of curiosity, determination, open-mindedness and so on. (See Section 5.4.1.)

ASK Model: the ASK Model is a development of Bloom's Taxonomy of Educational Objectives. It brings together a focus on **A**ttitudes, **S**kills and **K**nowledge. (See Section 5.4.)

Coaching: an approach to instruction that questions, challenges, encourages and guides the learner. (See Step 5 of the Seven Steps to Feedback in Section 7.1.)

Concept: a general idea that groups things together according to accepted characteristics.

Culture: the behaviors and beliefs that characterize a group of people. Used in the context of developing a positive culture for feedback. (See Chapter 3.)

Feedback: feedback should help students answer three key questions: What am I trying to achieve? How much progress have I made so far? What should I do next?

Feedforward: a term used by many people to emphasize the role of feedback in helping students plan forward and identify their next learning steps. (See Section 1.7.4.)

Formative Assessment: assessment that helps students "form" or identify their next steps in learning.

Grading: the awarding of a grade, mark or percentage. For example: A, B or C grade, or level 7, 6 or 5. (See Section 1.6.)

Knowledge: acquaintance with facts, truths or principles. Generally considered to be a step removed from understanding, which is when someone is able to relate, explain and evaluate.

Learning Focus: a learning focus includes an emphasis on questioning, challenging, striving to get better and beating personal bests. This is in contrast to a performance focus that hinges on grades, attainment and beating other people. (See Section 3.1.2.)

Learning Intention: a Learning Intention describes what students should know, understand or be able to do by the end of the lesson or series of lessons. (See Chapter 4.)

Metacognition: literally meaning "thinking about thinking," metacognition is an important part of feedback. It encourages students to think about *how* they are giving and receiving feedback as well as *what* the feedback messages are.

Peer Review: feedback that is given from one student to another.

Performance Focus: a performance focus hinges on grades, attainment and beating other people. This is in contrast to a learning focus that emphasizes questioning, challenging and beating personal bests. (See Section 3.1.2.)

Preview: gives students an idea about what they will be learning in advance of the lesson. This allows them to prepare beforehand. The effect can be significantly positive. (See Section 4.2.6.)

Process: the actions that lead to the learning goal. Focusing on process is particularly important when teaching students *how* to learn as much as *what* to learn.

Reflection: giving serious thought or consideration to a thought, idea or response.

Repertoire and Judgment: teachers have a repertoire of learning strategies, with good judgment required to know when and how to use those strategies.

Self-Regulation: an ability to control impulses, plan strategically and act thoughtfully.

Self-Review: when a student gives himself or herself feedback.

Skills: the abilities to carry out those processes necessary for gaining understanding, completing tasks or performing in any given context.

SOLO Taxonomy: the Structure of Observed Learning Outcomes model describes levels of increasing complexity in the understanding of subjects, originally proposed by John Biggs and Kevin Collis.

Success Criteria: the key steps or ingredients students need to accomplish the Learning Intention. They include the main things to do, include or focus on.

Summative Assessment: evaluation of the end result. It says what a student has been able to do. It is in contrast to formative assessment that identifies what a student could do next.

Taxonomy: a classification representing the intended outcomes of the educational process. (See Chapter 5.)

Tutorials: intensive instruction for an individual student or a small group of students. (See Section 2.3.3.)

Understanding: mental process of a person who comprehends. It includes an ability to explain cause, effect and significance, and to understand patterns and how they relate to each other.

WAGOLL: good feedback begins with criteria that identify *What A Good One Looks Like*. (See Section 2.1.7.)

Wii-FM: useful shorthand for reminding teachers to think on behalf of their students: **W**hat's **I**n **I**t **F**or **M**e?

> "The effect of feedback on learning . . . suggests average percentiles on learning outcomes of between 50% and 83% improvement."
>
> (Hattie, 2009)

SETTING THE SCENE

1.0 • WHY READ YET ANOTHER BOOK ABOUT FEEDBACK?

Your students construct meaning through relevant learning activities. The learning effects of these activities are largely determined by the type, amount and timing of feedback. It's as simple and as complex as that. High-quality feedback makes a significant difference to learning.

And yet, isn't everyone in education already giving students lots of feedback? Of course they are! Indeed, if feedback is information that helps shape the next action, then any raised eyebrow, nod, wink, or a corrective or cautionary murmur can be thought of as feedback. Put it like that and it becomes almost impossible to think of a lesson that is not filled with dollops of feedback. That is not to say all students receive and act upon the feedback constructively, of course, but it is there nonetheless.

So why should you read yet another book about feedback? Here are two reasons:

1. Everyone in education is already using feedback, yet very few of us are managing to use feedback well enough to double the rate of learning (which is what research identifies as the expected effect).

2. Despite the growing body of evidence advising otherwise, there are still too many outdated practices being used.

These are some feedback practices that need to change:

- mixing feedback with grades

> Feedback is information that helps to shape the next action.

> Research suggests that feedback doubles the rate of learning.

> And yet most students who receive feedback do not make double progress. Why not?

Some of the reasons are to do with the timing and type of feedback.

- assessing the quality of the feedback *given* rather than the effect of feedback received and applied

- assuming that feedback ought to be written when in fact it is best generated in dialogue with students

- giving feedback *after* students complete their learning rather than before (no, this is not cheating, as we will show in Chapter 7)

This book will show you what can be done about all of these.

1.0.1 • Research Evidence About Feedback

Feedback is central to student learning. This has been confirmed by a number of influential meta-analyses, including by Hattie, Biggs and Purdie (1996).

Paul Ramsden (2003) argues that effective comments on students' work represent one of the key characteristics of quality teaching.

Dai Hounsell (2003, p. 67) notes that "it has long been recognized, by researchers and practitioners alike, that feedback plays a decisive role in learning and development, within and beyond formal educational settings. We learn faster, and much more effectively, when we have a clear sense of how well we are doing, and what we might need to do in order to improve."

Some of the best-known research comes from Dylan Wiliam and Paul Black. In the 1990s in the United Kingdom, one of the most talked-about books among teachers was *Inside the Black Box* by Black and Wiliam (1990). In this thinnest of books, the authors summarized more than 250 research studies, arguing that Assessment for Learning (or AfL, as became its popular abbreviation) "could do more to improve educational outcomes than almost any other investment in education" (p. 314).

Later, Avraham Kluger and Angelo DeNisi (1996), Jeffrey Nyquist (2003) and Robert Marzano (2007) all gave similar evidence. Perhaps best known of all, John Hattie, of *Visible Learning* fame, identified this evidence from Richard Lysakowski and Herbert Walberg:

Myths about feedback:

- All feedback is good.

- Feedback should be given at the end of the learning process.

- Grades help with the feedback process.

All of these myths are misleading and sometimes completely untrue.

> **At least 12 previous meta-analyses have included specific information on feedback in classrooms. These meta-analyses included 196 studies and 6,972 effect sizes. The average effect was 0.79 (twice the average effect). To place this average of 0.79 into perspective, it fell in the top 5 to 10 highest influences on achievement. . . . Clearly, feedback can be powerful. (Hattie, Biggs & Purdie, 1996)**

However, it has not been all plain sailing. Despite—or maybe because of—its popularity, feedback and Assessment for Learning have fallen prey to overhype. Through a combination of gimmicks, government initiatives, simplistic messages and confusing policies, AfL has become at times a kind of *reductio ad absurdum*.

Some of the myths that have been pedaled include the following:

- All feedback is good.

- All lessons must start with success criteria.

- The time for feedback is during the "plenary" session at the end of each lesson.

- Grades and levels are feedback (and since all feedback is good, grades and levels are therefore good).

- Grades or "curriculum levels" will tell students where they are and what they need to do next.

- Turning students' achievements into numbers will make the process of learning easier to understand and therefore easier to improve.

- Feedback should be written down so that there is "proof" that feedback has been given.

These are just a few of the misinterpretations and oversimplifications that have developed over the years.

They are all entirely wrong or partly wrong.

With this book, we will help you avoid these pitfalls and problems. As teachers in the United Kingdom, we have encountered all of these problems; our government has mandated us to use them; even our school leaders have insisted we use them or risk "failing" as a teacher.

With this book, we hope to help you avoid these problems before it's too late!

1.1 • WHAT IS FEEDBACK?

Feedback is information we receive that helps to shape our next response. It can be formal or informal.

Someone who tells a joke is looking for feedback. When students show a teacher their work, they are looking for feedback. If someone touches something too hot, feedback comes in the form of pain. When two microphones amplify each other, the loud squeal is feedback.

Though these examples vary in degrees of formality, they all provoke responses: the joker tells another funny story, the students edit their work, the casualty removes the hand from the heat and the musician separates the microphones as quickly as possible.

However, when it comes to feedback in education, the process is very often overformalized. Indeed, many students seem to believe that feedback has to come from their teacher and that the feedback has to be written down and accompanied by a grade or score. And yet this is a mistake.

> Feedback flows all around a classroom. A nod, a wink, a yawn, a point or a cough can all be regarded as feedback.

Instead, it is much better to think of feedback as *any* message—formal or informal, verbal or nonverbal, written or spoken—that helps shape the receiver's next response. Thinking about it in this way will make it much more likely that feedback becomes an integral and everyday part of the learning process.

1.1.1 • Sources of Feedback

Feedback can come from many different sources: other people, books, games, experiences and self. A peer can suggest an alternative strategy, a book can give information that clarifies ideas, a parent can provide encouragement and support, a student can evaluate his or her own success and we can teach our students how to learn from all of these. All of this can influence the receiver's next response.

Winne and Butler (1994) offer an excellent summary in the *International Encyclopaedia of Education*: "Feedback is information with which a learner can confirm, add to, overwrite, tune, or restructure information in memory, whether that information is domain knowledge, meta-cognitive knowledge, beliefs about self and tasks, or cognitive tactics and strategies" (p. 5740).

1.1.2 • Receiving Feedback

Despite coming from many different sources, feedback is often not received or understood. David Carless (2006) found that students often find teachers' feedback confusing, non-reasoned and difficult to understand. Sometimes they think they have understood the teacher's feedback when they have not, and even when they do understand it they may not know how to use it.

Richard Higgins (2000, para. 4) argued that "many students are simply unable to understand feedback comments and interpret them correctly." And, as many of us know, some students find feedback intimidating even when it is well intentioned and communicated effectively.

Maddalena Taras (2003) suggests that a part of the problem is that teachers (and students) see feedback in isolation from other aspects of the teaching and learning process, and consider feedback to be primarily a teacher-owned endeavor.

Furthermore, Mary Sully de Luque and Steven Sommer (2000) found students from different cultures receive feedback in different ways. They discovered that students from collectivist cultures (e.g., Confucian-based Asian and South Pacific nations) prefer indirect and implied feedback relating to a group rather than to an individual, whereas students from individualistic cultures (e.g., the United States) prefer more direct, individualized feedback, particularly when related to effort. They also found individualistic students are more likely to engage in self-help strategies because this helps them gain status and achieve outcomes.

1.1.3 • Feedback Complexity

> **As Mantz Yorke (2003) argued in his examination of formative assessment, teachers need an awareness of the psychology of giving and receiving feedback as well as an understanding of the content of feedback.**

Furthermore, David Carless (2006) stated that feedback can have multiple functions: advice for the improvement of the current assignment, advice for the improvement of future assignments, explaining or justifying a grade, or an act by which the teacher demonstrates characteristics such as expertise, diligence or authority. He went on to say that students, and even teachers themselves, may not be fully aware of which of these functions or which combination of them is being enacted.

As teachers, we are not simply appraising our students' performance on a task, but we are also often looking for opportunities to teach or reinforce certain behaviors. Indeed, when giving feedback we may be fulfilling many different roles simultaneously: teacher, proofreader, editor, gatekeeper, life coach, encourager, evaluator, assessor, mentor and guide.

Feedback is information with which a student can confirm, add to, overwrite or fine-tune thoughts and/or actions.

Different students prefer different types of feedback.

Feedback is complex. That's why this book has been written: to help find a way through the maze!

In addition, our personal knowledge of our students is usually greater than it would be between, say, a book reviewer and an author or between an interviewer and an interviewee. Furthermore, we tend to have more interest in creating and maintaining a good relationship with our students than other people who offer feedback might have. This puts us in the position of having to weigh all sorts of (sometimes conflicting) needs all at the same time. For example: Is the short-term pain worth the long-term gain? How can I say this without demotivating my students? Is this a "battle" I need to lose so as to win the "war"? By saying the same thing to this student as I did to another student, will I undermine the sense that this feedback is personalized?

In other words, as teachers we often have to weigh our choice of comments to accomplish a range of informational, pedagogical and interpersonal goals simultaneously.

1.1.4 • Negative Feedback

According to Richard Higgins, Peter Hartley and Alan Skelton (2001), students are often dissatisfied with the feedback they receive in terms of lacking specific advice to improve, being difficult to interpret or having a potentially negative impact on students' self-perception and confidence.

In addition, some types of feedback are a lot less powerful than others. Feedback that comes in the form of praise or reward is among the least effective. Indeed, tangible rewards such as stickers and achievement awards contain such little task information that they shouldn't really be thought of as feedback—even though many teachers and students regard them as such.

> In their meta-analysis of the effects of feedback on motivation, Edward Deci, Richard Koestner and Richard Ryan (1999) found a negative correlation between extrinsic rewards and learning (–0.34). They also found that tangible rewards actually undermined intrinsic motivation, particularly for interesting tasks (–0.68), although they did find a small positive effect when the students were engaged in uninteresting tasks (0.18).

So perhaps when we think there is a need to motivate our students with extrinsic rewards, then it says more about the quality of the task we're asking them to complete than it does about the attitude or behavior of our students!

Note: The figures quoted from Deci et al. (1999) refer to effect sizes. Many researchers use effect size to show the relative effect of a strategy when compared with other strategies in the same field. John Hattie and many other researchers, including Dylan Wiliam and Shirley Clarke, have found that the average effect size of strategies used to help students learn is 0.4. So anything in the range 0.0 to 0.4 is positive but less than average; anything more than 0.4 is above average (and therefore relatively significant). And anything below zero has a negative effect on student learning.

Kluger and DeNisi (1996) conducted the most systematic meta-analysis on the effects of various types of feedback. Many of their studies focused on groups outside of typical schooling, for example, after-school clubs. So we're not just talking learning in classrooms here. From the 131 studies involving 12,652 participants, Kluger and DeNisi found the average effect of feedback was 0.38. This effect size is about average when compared with *all* effects on learning and therefore contrasts strongly with the headline that "feedback is one of the most powerful influences on student learning." One explanation for this is that of the 470 effects they found in those studies, 32 percent

Sometimes feedback can cause a negative effect—not just on students' mood but also on their learning outcomes.

Out of 131 studies, Kluger and DeNisi (1996) found one-third showed that feedback produced negative effects on student learning.

of them were negative. So in one-third of all cases, the feedback the students received actually caused them to make *less* progress than they would have done otherwise!

But is it really very surprising that some feedback is negative? Think about the feedback you've received in your life: Has it always helped you grow and develop? Or has it annoyed you or even put you off from ever trying again? That's the thing: surely it's silly to say "all feedback is good" since we know from bitter experience it is not.

Here's what Kluger and DeNisi (1996) found: when the feedback focused primarily on what the students had done wrong, or it was related to complex tasks that the students hadn't got their head around yet, and/or it threatened their self-esteem by making them feel as if they couldn't complete the task, then the feedback they received had a negative effect on their learning. Added to this, many of the types of feedback had very small effects and were therefore relatively ineffectual. These included praise for performance and extrinsic rewards.

1.1.5 • Top Three Feedback Questions

Feedback should provide information (relating to task, process or strategy) that helps your students close the gap between where they want to be next and where they are now.

To do this, feedback should help your students do the following:

1. Understand the goal or learning intention

2. Know where they are in relation to the goal

3. Realize what they need to do to bridge the gap between their current position and the goal

> **To put it another way, feedback should help learners answer these three questions:**
>
> 1. **What am I trying to achieve?**
> 2. **How much progress have I made so far?**
> 3. **What should I do next?**

1.1.6 • Feedback Checklist

This checklist shows some of the best ways to ensure that feedback has a positive effect.

Feedback needs to meet as many of the following criteria as possible:

- Feedback should relate to clear, specific and appropriately challenging goals.

- Students should be actively involved in the feedback process—not just passive recipients.

- Feedback is more effective when it helps your students identify what they have done correctly so that they can better identify for themselves what they could do next.

- Feedback should reduce uncertainty in relation to how well your students are performing on a task and what needs to be accomplished to attain the goal(s).

- Feedback should relate to the task, process and/or strategy; it should not be focused on the person.

- Feedback should be timely: coming *after* the initial teaching and first attempt but *before* your students finish their learning.

- Your students should be expected to use the feedback they receive.

- Feedback should answer the three key questions: What am I trying to achieve? How much progress have I made so far? What should I do next?

- Grading should be kept separate from feedback.

- Feedback should be unbiased and objective. Feedback from a trustworthy source will be considered more seriously than other feedback, which may be disregarded.

- Feedback should allow for learning from mistakes rather than making students fearful of failure.

- The quality of feedback should be judged not on what is given but on what effect it has. In other words, don't give feedback just to prove you have given it; instead, look for the effect of the feedback on the improvements in your students' performance and understanding.

- Feedback should not only be thought of as the information we give to our students; it should also be the information they get from books, parents, peers and themselves.

- Feedback can be used to move your students' attention away from a focus on performance and more toward a focus on learning. This includes emphasizing that effort leads to increased learning and that mistakes are an important part of the learning process.

- Feedback should be given in a culture of trust, respect and support.

1.2 • ASSESSMENT: TO SIT BESIDE

Often, the term *feedback* is used when giving advice to our students, whereas *assessment* is used when we are identifying (or measuring) what "level" students have reached. Ironic, then, that the word *assessment* has its roots in the Latin verb *assidere,* meaning "to sit beside"—which seems a long way removed from the practice of testing!

> *Assessment has its roots in the Latin verb assidere, meaning "to sit beside."*

The "sitting beside" form of assessment is the best way to engage your students in the feedback process. It makes feedback more collaborative and constructive. By sitting beside your students (whether literally or metaphorically), you should be able to better understand what and why they've done what they've done so far and what they might be able to do to improve. Perhaps more importantly, this sitting beside should also enable and encourage your students to take responsibility for directing and regulating their own learning.

The following are the sorts of details we might try to ascertain while sitting beside our students:

1. **Do they understand what they are trying to achieve?**

    This would usually include finding out:

    1. What they think the learning goal and the success criteria are (see Chapter 4)

    2. Which success criteria they believe are the most important

Here are some questions to ask when "sitting beside" students:

1. Do they understand what they are trying to achieve?

2. How much progress do they think they've made already?

3. What are some of the things they are thinking of doing next?

3. Which parts of the learning journey are the most challenging and why

4. Whether there are any success criteria they think could be added to help them reach their learning goal

2. How much progress do they think they've made already?

It would be good to find out what your students think of the following:

1. How much progress they think they've made so far

2. How "far" from their learning goal are they at the moment

3. How satisfied they are with the steps they've already taken

4. Whether they think they've covered all the success criteria as well as they might have done

3. What are some of the things they are thinking of doing next?

The following questions should help your students identify for themselves what they might do next:

1. What is one thing you could do to improve what you've already done?

2. What could you add to what you've already done that will improve the quality of your learning so far?

3. Which parts of the success criteria do you still need to attend to so that you reach your learning goal?

4. Is there a different way of looking at what you're trying to do or a different strategy that you could use that would help you make even more progress?

5. What attitudes, skills or knowledge could you take from this task that could help you with future learning?

Things to Notice About These Questions

Education comes from the Latin verb *educere,* meaning "to draw out." This fits nicely with these questions and with the process of sitting beside our students to draw out their ideas and understanding.

Asking your students what *they* think rather than telling them what to do next should, over time, help them become more assessment capable (see Chapter 7).

We have included questions related to strategy and process as well as to content.

1.3 • FOUR LEVELS OF FEEDBACK

John Hattie and Helen Timperley (2007) classified feedback in terms of four levels, noting how the different types of feedback interacted with particular types of tasks.

Level 1: Task-Related

Task-related feedback is the most common form of feedback in schools. It generally relates to specific criteria within the task. For example:

> "The task was to measure the length of all three sides of the triangle, but you have only shown one measurement so far."

"Check sentences 2, 4 and 7 as they're missing capital letters and/or periods."

"Munich is not the capital of Germany and the population is much higher than 1.4 *thousand*! Check these stats before continuing."

Task-related feedback is often known as "corrective feedback." It is particularly useful for beginners to help them build (or correct) surface-level knowledge. It can also be the springboard for higher forms of feedback such as process or self-regulation feedback.

Beware, however, of using task-related feedback indiscriminately! Most feedback to whole classes is at this task-related level, and yet, because it tends to be specific (and therefore not particularly generalizable), many students frequently dismiss it as irrelevant to them.

Level 2: Process-Related

Process-related feedback is much more effective than task-level feedback for deepening learning and creating understanding. It generally relates to the process of learning:

- reassessment of the approach being used

- thinking of alternative strategies for task analysis or completion

- trying different methods of error detection

- more efficient or more comprehensive methods for information gathering

- strategies for making tasks more manageable or achievable

Level 3: Self-Regulation

Self-regulation feedback comes from students monitoring their own thoughts and actions. It is the feedback they give themselves in terms of reaffirming what their goal is and whether they are still on course, considering whether there is a better process they could use, seeking feedback at appropriate moments, deciding how to deal with feedback information and so on.

Self-regulation feedback can do the following:

- enhance self-evaluation skills

- generate greater confidence to engage further in the task

- help decide what to do for the best outcome

When your students self-regulate their own learning, they will become more independent learners. Self-regulation requires students to be metacognitive, self-motivated and active in their own learning.

Level 4: Self-Related

The final type of feedback—related to self—does not build on the other forms of feedback, so we've referred to it simply as "another" level. Furthermore, this self-feedback can impact negatively on learning, whereas the other three can create a positive progression toward deeper understanding.

Feedback directed to the self refers to comments about the individual, for example, "you're very clever" or "you're not very good at this." Comments such as these can put students into what Carol Dweck calls a *fixed mindset*.

Hattie and Timperley (2007) found four types of feedback:

1. Task-related

2. Process-related

3. Self-regulation

4. Self-related

Feedback that is related to the person can have a negative impact on learning and thus should be avoided.

1.4 • MATCHING FEEDBACK TO LEVELS OF UNDERSTANDING (USING THE SOLO TAXONOMY)

> The SOLO taxonomy provides a useful framework for matching feedback to a student's stage of learning.

The SOLO taxonomy is a model that was proposed by John Biggs and Kevin Collis in 1982. SOLO stands for the Structure of Observed Learning Outcomes. It is a means of classifying learning in terms of its complexity, which in turn helps to identify the quality and depth of students' understanding.

The SOLO taxonomy is covered in depth in Chapter 6. For now, Figure 1 presents a brief overview of how feedback can be matched to levels of understanding.

▶ Figure 1: Verbs Associated With the SOLO Taxonomy

SOLO Level	Feedback Verbs
Prestructural *Has no idea*	*Too soon for feedback, as direct instruction is needed first.*
Unistructural *Has one idea*	find, match, label, name, list
Multistructural *Has many ideas*	describe, define, combine, follow, identify a pattern
Relational *Understands the whole*	classify, analyze, relate, apply, explain, organize
Extended Abstract *Predicts and invents*	evaluate, prioritize, hypothesize, create an analogy

1.5 • PRAISE VS. FEEDBACK

> Praise is not the same as feedback.

Praise is not the same as feedback. Feedback answers all three of the questions mentioned before: What am I trying to achieve? How much progress have I made so far? What should I do next? Praise, on the other hand, tends only to focus on what students have done well so far.

That is not to say that praise is a bad thing. Praise might put students in a better mood or give them an indication that we appreciate them. However, it is very rarely converted into a desired outcome such as more engagement, commitment to learning, enhanced self-efficacy or understanding about the task.

That is also not to say your students won't *like* praise: they almost certainly will. P. R. Sharp (1985) reported that 26 percent of the adolescent students in his sample preferred to be praised loudly and publicly when they achieved on an academic task, 64 percent preferred to be praised quietly and privately and only 10 percent preferred teachers to say nothing at all.

Paul Burnett (2002) reported similar results among younger students and found that students preferred praise for trying hard rather than for having a high ability (especially when the praise was public) and for achievement rather than for behavior.

On the other hand, if the culture of the peer group is "it's not cool to try," then that very same praise can be seen as punishment.

Furthermore, praise might be counterproductive and have negative consequences on students' self-evaluations of their ability. Wulf-Uwe Meyer (1982) found that older students perceived praise after success or neutral feedback after failure as an indication that the teacher perceived their ability to be low. When given criticism after failure and neutral feedback after success, they perceived that the teacher had estimated their ability to be high and their effort low.

It is important, however, to distinguish between praise that directs attention to the student and praise directed to the effort, self-regulation, engagement or processes relating to the learning. This latter type of praise can assist in enhancing self-efficacy and can therefore help with the learning process.

Part of the reason for the unpredictability of praise is that students often adopt "reputational lenses" to seek or evaluate feedback. For example, some students might want to be seen as good students, whereas others might want to achieve the exact opposite. According to Goethals, Messick and Allison (1991), "Students do a lot of 'in the head' comparisons and it is likely that such comparisons are selected, interpreted and/or biased. Strengths and positive performances are seen as unique and self-created, whereas weakness and negative performances are seen as common in others and possibly caused by others."

With all that said, feedback *is* more powerful when it is personalized. That is not to say it should be focused on the person (for example, "You are a clever student" or "Good boy, you've done well"). But when you engage personally with your students, then you acknowledge them as fellow human beings with things to say and thoughts and interests of their own.

Phrases such as these might help:

- What you did there was very powerful.
- That was a moving performance.
- What you've written here is interesting.
- You make a significant point.
- This made me laugh/think/wonder.
- I learned something about this topic from you.
- I learned something about your interests.
- I never thought about that before.
- It's interesting that you think X. Have you ever thought about Y?

> Sometimes praise can have a negative effective on learning. This is particularly true if students perceive it as an indication that their teachers are surprised by the students' success.

1.6 • DOES GRADING COUNT AS FEEDBACK?

When we give students a grade, the learning stops. When we give students specific feedback and an extending question, the learning goes deeper.

It is a well-rehearsed argument that grades do very little for the learning process. Indeed, as Ruth Butler and others have pointed out, grades often diminish the power of feedback to the point that giving feedback together with grades is the equivalent of giving no feedback at all.

Butler (1997) split 132 eleven-year-olds into three groups. The first group was given comments only, the second group was given grades only and the third group was given what most students are given: grades and comments. She then looked at how much additional gain each group made as a result of this information they had been given.

▶ **Figure 2: The Effect of Grades on Learning Outcomes**

Group	Feedback	Sometimes Shown	Mostly Shown
A	Comments only	30% Gain	Positive
B	Grades only	No Gain	Top 25% - Positive Bottom 25% - Negative
C	Grades and Comments	No Gain	Top 25% - Positive Bottom 25% - Negative

As Figure 2 shows, the group that received only comments made an additional 30 percent gain in their learning. The group that received only grades made no additional gain. The worrying part, though, is that the students who received grades and comments made no additional gain!

Remember that feedback should tell your students what they have done well *and* what they should do next. Grades alone cannot tell them this. But when you put grades with comments, too many students will look at their grades first and, if it is a good grade, think to themselves, "Why do I need to improve?" And if they've got a bad grade, then they think, "Why try to improve? I'm no good at this anyway!"

This theme is also explored by Black and Wiliam in "Working Inside the Black Box" (Black, Harrison, Lee, Marshall & Wiliam, 1990). Teacher-feedback should normally avoid giving marks. Research experiments have established that while pupils' learning can be advanced by feedback through comments, the giving of marks, or grades, has a negative effect in that pupils ignore comments when marks are also given.

> And yet, like so many teachers, I was expected, when I was a teacher, to give marks or grades whenever I responded to a pupil's work. When I stopped this practice, many of my students questioned whether something was wrong. Some of their parents complained I wasn't marking properly—and even one or two heads of department advised me to return to standard practice as soon as possible.
>
> Over time, though, my students did begin to read my comments and feedback more thoroughly. When I asked them why this was, they reported that previously, if they got 10 out of 10 or an A or B grade, then there was no point reading my comments because they knew they'd done well. Or, if they'd got a low grade or score, then they knew that they were useless, so what was the point in reading any further? (Black & Wiliam, 2002)

In the Seven Steps to Feedback we show you how you can make grading more useful. We show you that keeping grades separate from the comments and getting your students to

Black and Wiliam found that grades have a negative effect on students' learning.

If you feel obliged to give grades, then keep them separate from feedback. The Seven Steps to Feedback in Chapter 7 go into this in depth.

grade their own work will have a much greater impact than grading usually does. Indeed, if you tell your students at the beginning of a task that they will be expected to grade their own work at the end, then they will probably take much more notice of the success criteria! So perhaps grading can be put to good effect after all?

We will explore the Seven Steps to Feedback in depth in Chapter 7.

1.7 • OTHER TYPES OF FEEDBACK

Deciding on the best form of feedback will depend on context, but using the types that follow, when appropriate, will enrich your lessons.

1.7.1 • Coaching

Coaching is a form of intensive, planned encouragement and guidance targeted at developing essential skills, positive attitudes and other personal resources for life and learning. It is based on the principle of one person actively seeking feedback from a person they trust, respect and want feedback from and then receiving it in the form of guided dialogue.

1.7.2 • Dialogue

> **Dialogue is the most immediate and collaborative way of giving feedback to your students. It provides both a stimulus and a model for their own reflections on learning as well as their strategies for understanding.**

Dialogue is more than just speaking and listening—it is the very foundation for thinking. Lev Vygotsky, George Herbert Mead and, more recently, Matthew Lipman, have all argued in broad terms:

- Tasks we can jointly accomplish by talking together are gradually internalized so they become tasks we can achieve independently through our own thinking.

- Thinking is rather like an internal dialogue. If we are exposed to rich, reflective dialogue, then characteristics of dialogue such as question and response manifest themselves in our own thinking, helping us become more reflective.

- Recognizing the significance of this internal dialogue is an important step in improving the quality of feedback and, therefore, of learning.

This is explored far more in *Challenging Learning Through Dialogue* (Nottingham, Nottingham & Renton, 2016).

> Feedback too often leaves students unsure about exactly what they have done well and what they can do to improve.

1.7.3 • Editing

Feedback is not the same as editing. Feedback to your students should provide them with a clear message about how to improve their performance without simply doing it for them (as editing might).

Feedback is about guidance. Diagnosis of what is wrong can be part of the process, but it should be accompanied by clear suggestions for improvement, for example, "Here's what's wrong and here are some suggestions for ways to fix it."

Compare this with a study by Melanie Weaver (2006) in which she found that most students complained the feedback they received was too general and vague with no suggestions for improvement. The students reported that they were often left not knowing what they had done well, what they needed to change and why they had achieved the grade they had.

1.7.4 • Feedback and Feedforward

Feedback is not just about looking *back*. It is also about looking *forward* and thinking about possible next steps. Some people like to use the term *feedforward*. The problem is that this suggests feed*back* does not include looking forward, but it does and it should. Indeed, this book will show that feedback *has* to look forward as well as back if it is to be the hugely powerful influence on learning that research tells us it can be.

Having said that, Deirdre Burke (2009) discovered that many students "interpret the term 'feedback' literally and use it only to look back on work they have completed, and are not aware or able to use teacher comments to 'feed-forward' and contribute to their on-going development."

This makes it even more important to emphasize to your students that feedback needs to answer *all three* questions: What am I trying to achieve? How much progress have I made so far? What should I do next?

1.7.5 • Formative and Summative Assessment

Formative assessment is feedback that provides explanation, diagnosis, prompting and/or elaboration to your students in response to their efforts. Formative assessment enables them to make further progress. Usually, a complete form of feedback is dialogue.

Summative feedback identifies only what the students have done right and what they have done wrong. It usually involves a grade or exit rating.

Figure 3 shows the main differences.

> Formative feedback helps to form the next steps. Summative feedback gives a summary of what has been achieved so far.

▶ **Figure 3: Different Types of Formative and Summative Assessment**

Confimation	Your answer was right/wrong.	Summative Assessment
Corrective	Your answer was incorrect. The right answer is . . .	
Explanatory	Your answer was incorrect because . . .	Formative Assessment
Diagnostic	Your answer suggests you forgot to . . . Next time, concentrate on the following before answering.	
Elaborative	Your answer was spot on. A key to this was your decision to focus on . . . To improve even more next time, I suggest you . . .	

An example of formative assessment would look something like this:

Learning goal: To make better use of examples and counter-examples in writing so that the conclusion is more considered.

Teacher's comments: "Well done, Craig. You have made significant progress toward reaching the learning goal. There are now far more wide-ranging and thought-provoking examples to support your conclusions than in your earlier work. I particularly like the example you used in line 7 that suggests common sense isn't always right. What I'd like to see more of now is the use of counter-examples, as these will help to create a less biased tone to your conclusion."

Questions to think about: "Can you think of two or three counter-examples that would persuade you to rethink your conclusion? Which one is the most persuasive? Where would that best fit within your answer? What would be some of the benefits of using counter-arguments in your writing?"

(Martin Renton) When I first started working on feedback in my classroom, trying to understand the difference between formative and summative assessment was vital in order to make any changes to my practice. But it was a longer process than I expected.

My colleagues who initially explained it described summative feedback as "coming at the end," whereas formative feedback would happen "during the lesson." This simplistic definition was easy to understand initially but, like all simple definitions, is actually rather misleading and therefore difficult to implement. As I found out, it is not really about when to assess; it is more about *how* you assess and, of course, *why* you are assessing.

Traditionally the teacher has been perceived as the expert, having all the answers. When students are working on a task, it is too easy to give feedback on what they have done right or wrong and then tell them what the answer really is. Even if this happens in the middle of a lesson, it is still summative assessment, as it prevents the continuation of learning.

Equally, there were countless occasions in my early teaching career when I collected in the final piece of work at the end of a module, graded it, explained why that grade was given and then set a target on how to improve it next time. When of course there is no next time! And so the feedback was meaningless.

Angela Stockton (2015) defines formative assessment as a verb, rather than a noun. It is not a "thing that students are given to complete at the beginning, in the middle, or at the end" of the learning experience (para. 3), it is an action performed throughout it. Because of this, she describes feedback as the "by-product of formative assessment done right," whereas grades are the "by-product of formative assessment gone horribly wrong" (para. 11).

From these early experiences, I learned two things:

1. Feedback will have more impact when it is focused on helping your students learn for themselves rather than if you tell them what is right and what is wrong.

2. When we grade formative assessments (during the learning process), rather than asking the three important questions, we are effectively penalizing students for having not mastered something they are still learning about.

The following analogy has helped me picture the difference between formative and summative assessment and helped me make changes to my practice over time:

Imagine you plant a sunflower and wish it to grow to a meter tall. You plant the seed in a pot and water it every few days for three months.

> Formative feedback is better thought of as a verb rather than a noun. In other words, it should involve action rather than an award or penalty.

Summative assessment would mean that at the end of the three months, you would measure the sunflower and report if it has achieved or failed to reach the desired height.

Formative assessment would mean that you would constantly check on the flower's progress throughout the three months, support its growth by adding new soil, water more or less regularly according to its need, add plant feed, move the pot to give it more light and so on.

Summative assessment tells you what has been achieved in the past. Formative assessment underpins your decision making to enable you to best help it to flourish.

1.7.6 • Peer and Self-Reviews

Graham Nuthall (2007) conducted extensive in-class observations and noted that 80 percent of the verbal feedback students receive on a day-to-day basis comes from their peers and most of it is incorrect!

That said, students *can* be taught how to give better feedback to their peers. To do this, they need to be aware of their learning goals, understand success criteria and recognize good performances. Furthermore, receiving feedback from peers can lead to positive effects relating to reputation as learners, success and reduction of uncertainty, but it can also have the opposite effect if done badly. This is explored in Chapters 3 and 7.

1.7.7 • Student-to-Teacher Feedback

Learning is more powerful when you welcome feedback from your students about what they have understood, where they are conscious of making mistakes and when they are engaged. Such openness will make it clear to your students that feedback is important for everyone, teachers included (see also Section 2.3.7).

> Most of the feedback that students receive during the day comes from other students, and most of it is wrong! This makes it vitally important to teach students *how* to generate high-quality, accurate feedback.

1.8 • REVIEW

This chapter has covered the following main points:

1. Feedback is central to student learning. This has been confirmed by a number of influential meta-analyses, including those by Hattie et al. (1996), Black and Wiliam (1998) and Hattie and Jaeger (1998).

2. Some myths about feedback continue to be pedaled, whereas the truth of the matter is that *not* all feedback is good, feedback should not *only* occur at the end of the lesson or piece of work, feedback does *not* require a grade and feedback does *not* need to be written down.

3. Feedback is *any* message—formal or informal, verbal or nonverbal, written or spoken—that helps shape the receiver's next response.

4. Graham Nuthall (2007) noted that 80 percent of the verbal feedback students receive comes from their peers, and most of it is incorrect.

5. Feedback is most powerful when it is part of a dialogue between teacher and student. Indeed, the etymology of *assess* is "to sit beside."

6. Hattie and Timperley (2007) classified feedback in terms of four levels: task-related, process-related, self-regulated and self-related. They noted each type had a particular relevance at different stages in the learning process.

7. Feedback should help students (1) understand the goal or learning intention, (2) know where they are in relation to the goal and (3) realize what they need to do to bridge the gap between their current position and the goal they are striving for.

8. Different feedback is needed at different levels of understanding. The SOLO taxonomy can help to determine what is appropriate.

1.9 • NEXT STEPS

Here are some suggestions to help you with your reflections on feedback:

1. Pay attention to the types of feedback that take place in your classroom. Which interactions would you class as most useful to your students?

2. How do your students react to feedback? Are they generally positive and proactive toward it?

3. Are there some common features of feedback within different disciplines? For example, between feedback on written assignments compared to feedback toward active learning?

4. How often do you give personalized feedback to each of your students?

5. What are the benefits?

6. What problems do you encounter?

> "The first fundamental principle of effective classroom feedback is that feedback should be more work for the recipient than the donor."
>
> (Wiliam, 2011)

CURRENT REALITY

2.0 • WHAT IS YOUR FEEDBACK LIKE NOW?

Few practices promote learning more than personalized, well-timed, constructive feedback.

To help you identify how effective your feedback already is, you can use this chapter as a checklist to think about what you've already got in place. As you read through the list, keep asking yourself the three questions at the heart of good feedback:

- What am I trying to achieve?

- How much progress have I made so far?

- What can I do next?

2.1 • CHARACTERISTICS OF EXCELLENT FEEDBACK

The following is a checklist to help you identify how effective your feedback practices already are. It is not an exhaustive list, but it does identify some very important points about high-quality feedback.

This chapter shares a checklist for high-quality feedback.

2.1.1 • Ongoing Feedback

Learning loses its effectiveness when it is a one-off event rather than an ongoing process. Too often, though, students are given just one shot at an assignment and are then given a grade. This gives very little room for risk taking, experimentation and practice.

Instead, students should be given opportunities to close the gap between current and desired performance *during* the learning process. And a good way to achieve this is to give them feedback *before* they have completed their work.

Furthermore, by reviewing your students' work during the learning process, you will gain insight into their current level of understanding. This in turn gives you the chance to adjust content or pedagogy before the end of the unit of work.

This is covered in more depth in the Seven Steps to Feedback in Chapter 7.

2.1.2 • Feedback for ALL

Students who are struggling with their learning often receive better and more frequent feedback than those who are already doing very well. This may seem natural—and maybe even reasonable—but strong students are likely to suffer from this disproportionate attention.

Though it might be tempting to scrawl "Excellent!" on an advanced student's work and move on, this will not help that student gain insight into what they've done well and what they could do to enhance their performance. Even the best students need your guidance to improve. And of course, some might need that extra push to reach their potential—or even to go beyond it.

So make sure that all your students are receiving high-quality, well-timed and productive feedback.

2.1.3 • Timely Feedback

When it takes a week or two to get feedback to students, the flow of learning often breaks and students lose interest. On the other hand, prompt feedback guides students at a time when they can still recall what they did and *why* they did it. This significantly increases the motivation your students will have for improving their work.

In most cases, the sooner we give feedback to our students, the better. And yet it is not as simple as that. For a start, our students need time to complete their first draft (or first attempt), to receive feedback (from themselves or their peers) and then to edit their work. Only then should we get involved by giving them feedback. Jumping in any sooner will reduce our students' opportunity to develop their self-feedback and reflection skills. However, once draft two is complete, *then* the sooner we give our feedback, the better!

Remember: If we wait too long to give feedback, the moment can be lost and our students might not be able to connect the feedback to their original action. So wait until they've made their first attempt, received self or peer feedback and edited their work; then get in there as quickly as possible and give them some excellent advice to improve their performance even more!

2.1.4 • Consequential Feedback

Feedback is almost useless unless your students respond to it. As we all know, it is not uncommon to correct the same errors on some students' work over and over again. This may well be because those students are not taking your advice or are not being required to do so.

Feedback should be given during the learning process, not afterward.

Feedback should be given to all students, not just to those who are falling behind.

Feedback should be timed just right: not too soon (as this will prevent students from learning) and not too late (as this will reduce the chance of students making use of the feedback).

Effective feedback is concrete, specific and useful. And it provides *actionable* information. Comments such as "well done," "improve this" or "C+" are *not* examples of good feedback. Well done for what specifically? Improve what: the grammar, the tone, the conclusion or the clarity? And as for the grade, what action does that prompt (other than to be satisfied or disappointed)?

We need to take steps to make feedback more consequential. This is explored in more detail in the Seven Steps to Feedback (see Chapter 7) and includes color-coding edits, ensuring students receive feedback—from their peers, themselves or you—during the drafting process rather than at the end, "sitting beside" your students (whether literally or metaphorically) and engaging in a dialogue about their learning, and students chunking their work so that they have time to include recommendations from feedback in future iterations.

2.1.5 • Track Your Feedback

When you look over students' shoulders at the work they are doing, do you know what feedback you gave a particular student last time and what the target is to improve this time? If not, it will be harder to monitor whether students are taking your advice and acting on it or not. This might also lead to you repeating the same feedback to the same students again and again!

A simple monitoring system will help you keep track of the feedback you have given each of your students. This will make it much more likely that you can continue to give each student consequential feedback *during* the learning process so that it is timely, personal to that student and focused on progress.

This is also a good way to collect evidence about the amount of progress your students are making. As they achieve one target, the next target should move them forward in their learning and demonstrate that they are making progress.

2.1.6 • User-Friendly

Even if feedback is specific and accurate in your eyes, it is not of much value if your students cannot understand it or are overwhelmed by it. Highly technical feedback will seem odd and confusing to a novice. Describing a golf swing to a six-year-old in terms of torque and hip rotation is unlikely to improve the child's technique. Or telling an uninterested teenager to "sharpen your critique" rarely reaps dividends.

Neil Duncan (2007) found that the following common phrases used by teachers were some that students found difficult to interpret and act upon:

- Deepen analysis of key issues.
- Sharpen critique.
- Identify and develop implications.
- Link theory and practice.

Add these to the phrases often directed toward younger students, and we soon see the problems with feedback that is not specific, useful or understandable:

- Think about it.
- This does not make sense.
- Try harder.
- Pay attention to grammar and spellings.

> Feedback should always lead to action.

> Feedback should ensure that no students miss out or receive ill-suited messages.

> Feedback should be adapted so that the receiver can understand it and apply it thoughtfully.

- You have not listened well enough.

- Work together better.

- Good effort.

- Concentrate more.

- Great work.

The best advice, then, is to give specific, understandable and actionable feedback that will likely yield an immediate and noticeable improvement.

2.1.7 • WAGOLL

Good feedback begins with criteria that identify *What A Good One Looks Like* (WAGOLL). Some people call this *feedforward*—giving guidelines as to what success will look like. An agreed-upon set of criteria will increase your students' understanding of what is expected of them. This in turn gives them a better chance of performing well with the task.

A good way to share WAGOLL is to give your students two or three completed pieces of work and ask them to compare and contrast them. If for example, you show three pieces of work completed by a different group of students (with their names removed), then you could ask your current students to

- use the success criteria to identify which is the excellent piece, which is good and which is just average—and say why, or

- decide what the success criteria were that were used to make the judgments shown.

Compare this with a study by Dai Hounsell (1997), who found that teachers and students often had quite different conceptions about the goals and criteria for essays and that poor essay performance correlated with the degree of mismatch.

Remember also that your feedback should refer to the original criteria. There is little point in giving success criteria at the beginning of the learning process if you do not then make the very same criteria the focus of your feedback. By referring to these criteria, you will make your feedback transparent and fair. You will also give your students a *specific* sense of what they have achieved in progressing toward their goals and what they have yet to achieve.

2.1.8 • Goal-Referenced

Effective feedback requires your students to have a goal, take action to achieve the goal and receive goal-related information about their actions. The goal in telling a joke is to make people laugh. Writing a story with vivid language and believable dialogue that captures the characters' feelings is aimed at engaging the reader. The soccer player kicks a ball with the aim of gaining a competitive advantage. If any of the people engaging in these actions are not clear about their goals or if they fail to pay attention to them, they cannot get helpful feedback (nor are they likely to achieve their goals).

Information becomes feedback if, and only if, someone tries to do something and the information tells them whether they are on track or need to change course. If some joke or aspect of the writing *isn't working,* then the author needs to know!

In everyday situations, goals are often fairly obvious. Jokers don't need to announce when they're telling a joke for people to know their aim is to make people laugh (though some people need a heads-up to recognize irony!). It's pretty obvious when observing

> Feedback should help students understand What A Good One Looks Like (WAGOLL).

> Feedback should help achieve agreed-upon goals.

people ascending a climbing wall what their aim is. And most computer games have easily recognizable aims.

However, in school many students are often unclear about the specific goals of a task. So when giving feedback, make sure you refer to the goals and the criteria of the task. For example:

> The aim of this writing task is to describe an emotional roller coaster. So when rereading your draft or getting feedback from your response partner, check that you have described the varying emotions of your main character. At the moment, he seems pretty happy all the way through the story so far.

We have included lots of examples of Learning Intentions and Success Criteria in Chapter 4.

2.2 • CORRECTIVE, COMPONENT AND COMPREHENSIVE FEEDBACK

In Figure 3 (in Chapter 1) we identified five different types of feedback that make up formative and summative assessment. Another way to categorize feedback is into three Cs: corrective, component and comprehensive.

Corrective feedback is akin to proofreading and is generally focused on the mechanics or rules of something. For example, in a written piece of work, the rules would include spelling, grammar, punctuation and—for young children—word and letter formation. In science, it would include identifying factually incorrect statements or erroneous use of abbreviations. In sports, it would include the correction of any foul play or rule-breaking actions.

Component feedback is related to specific items or parts of a performance that do not break any "rules." For example, component feedback on a written piece of work might focus on the variety of adjectives used, the clarity of a sentence or the order in which paragraphs appear. In a history paper, it might look at diagrams used, theories proposed or conclusions drawn. Component feedback about swimming might focus on the position of the head or rhythm of the leg kicks; neither of them break any "rules" but could be changed as a way to, for example, improve efficiency, style or comfort.

Comprehensive feedback relates to the overall performance of something. In written work, this might focus on pace, style and tone—and whether the author has met all the success criteria. Other examples would include the clarity and justification of ideas in a spoken piece or the overall efficiency or aesthetic of a sporting performance.

Knowing the differences between these types of feedback can bring clarity to the feedback process. For example, it is always tempting to pick up on errors in grammar and spelling when reviewing a piece of written work. But, as we explore in Section 2.1.7 and Chapter 4, this can sometimes be distracting and very often disheartening to students. For example, if one of your students has tried their very best to write a really scary story filled with suspense and has just asked you for suggestions for making it even scarier, then they are likely to find it frustrating if all you pick up on is spelling and punctuation! Or if you have agreed with your students that the Learning Intentions and Success Criteria (see Chapter 4) are to do with adjectives, making good use of tenses and building up a description of the main characters, then that is what they will expect your feedback to be about, *not* punctuation, grammar and spelling. But then that leads many of us to worry that if we don't pick up on those mistakes, then we are in fact condoning sloppy writing!

> A useful way to think about feedback is in terms of corrective, component and comprehensive feedback.

> Knowing the difference between these three types of feedback can bring clarity to the whole process. It can also help prevent an overemphasis on corrective feedback.

That's where the distinctions between these three types of feedback can be useful: you can agree ahead of time which type you will be giving and why. You could say, for example, "I want you to give each other corrective feedback, ask me for component feedback and then in groups I'd like you to generate comprehensive feedback for each other."

Remember: all of these types of feedback can be useful. The problem is that many teachers overemphasize error correction, which can be disheartening for students, particularly when it comes in the form of red marks all over their work or when it breaks the flow of their performance.

So a good way to reduce the amount of error correction you give is to ask your students to take responsibility for it. Ask them to give each other error-corrective feedback in pairs. They should find it the easiest to generate, and it will begin to build their self and peer review abilities. As for the other two types of feedback, many teachers find it easier to give component feedback and yet most students prefer comprehensive feedback. This is partly because comprehensive feedback gives students fewer things to concentrate on but also because it tends to help them make more significant improvements to the overall quality of their work.

The key is to know the purpose for each type of feedback, to recognize who would benefit most from it and when, and to ask different people to generate the different types at different times. That way, all of your students should benefit.

Over the next few pages are examples of each of the three types of feedback.

▶ Figure 4: Example of Error-Correction Feedback

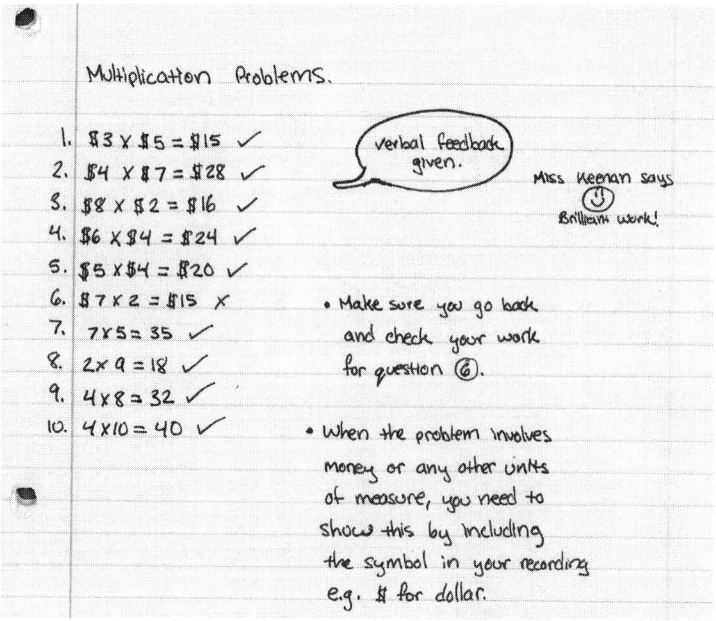

> Corrective feedback focuses on rules such as spelling or grammar and on "right" or "wrong" answers. This is often the form of feedback that students find easiest to give each other.

> Component feedback focuses on different components of the whole piece. It does not focus on spelling and grammar or right and wrong but instead looks at qualitative aspects such as effectiveness, style and aesthetics.

▶ Figure 5: Example of Component Feedback

Please note that in the following example, the teacher's questions and student's answers during the feedback session were spoken, not written. They are written here purely because this is a book! See Section 7.2 for an explanation of why the feedback was not written.

Student's Work	Teacher's Component Feedback Followed by Student's Verbal Responses

Student's Work

Air Resistance Experiment.

Learning objective
- To be able to predict and conclude giving reasons why.
- To understand the need to repeat measurements.
- To understand air resistance and its effects.

Key question
① Does the surface area ~~off~~ of the spinners wings effect the rate/speed at which it falls?

What Variable will I change
② The variable I will change is the Surface area on the wings.

What factors will I Keep the Same?
③
- The height you drop it from.
- The ~~wheight~~ weight of the paperclip.
- The part of the room/place where it dropped.
- The weight of the papper (how many paper)
- The person dropping it.

What will I measure?
④ I will measure the time it takes the Spinner to touch the floor.
To measure this the equipment I will use will be a Stop watch.

My prediction ⑤
I think the yellow Spinner is going to fall the slowest because it has more Surface area.
I think the blue Spinner is going to drop the quickest because it has less surface area.

Diagram: ⑥
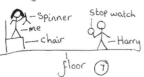
floor ⑦

Conclusion
The Spinner that fell most slowly was the yellow Spinner because it's ~~had 99cm~~ wings were 190cm². This is because it had more Surface area and therefore created the most air resistance.

The Spinner that fell most quickly was the blue Spinner because its wings were 99cm², this is because it had less Surface area and therefore created the least air resistance.
⑧
⑨

Teacher's Component Feedback Followed by Student's Verbal Responses

1. Using the same equipment, what other question could you investigate?

Whether the height at which it is dropped makes a difference or not.

2. Good choice of variable, Ava! What made you go for this?

I thought the wings would make the most difference.

3. Well done! You have listed many things that you will keep the same and only one thing you will change. This will make it a fair test.

Thanks!

4. How many measurements will you need to take?

If I've got time, then maybe three or four?

5. You have supported your prediction with good reasoning. Why else do you think your prediction is good?

I think the wings will make the biggest difference. That's why big airplanes have bigger wings than small airplanes.

6. A good clear diagram showing how you performed your experiment. What else could you add to make this even more accurate?

Height measurements, maybe?

7. Could you and Harry have swapped places?

No, because Harry is taller than me, so it would have further to fall.

8. Your conclusion links up with your prediction and has some good reasoning and explanation. Can you identify the key words you used to help you do this?

Because and therefore.

9. Can you explain why it was important to repeat the measurements, Ava?

Comprehensive feedback refers to the whole. It includes comments about the quality of the overall product or performance.

The Mystory Voice!!!

There once lived a yong 10 year old girl named Mable who lived an ordanary life until...

One early monday morning Mable was putting her brown thick hair up for School and suddenly, the phone rang So mable whent to pick it up before school. "Hello?" Mable asked nervously. "Hello" a deep Voice Said back to her "is this Mable?" the deep voice asked. "Yes it is, Why?" Mable asked even more nervously this time her knees were knocking together. "I need you at the haunted I mean comfoting School" the deep voice told her. "OK em e what time?" Mable asked "NOW!" the deep voice Shouted. "OK ok I'm coming!" Mable told him.

So Mable arrived at the School (the haunted School) "Hello, is anybody ahhh!" Mable cried. "Wwwhat happened?" Mable asked quite scared. "You my dear have fallen for my trap!" The same deep voice eccoed from along the corridoor "Wwhat trap?" Mable asked really scared now "The haunted school trap ofcourse." The deep voice replied gett loader and loader. "NO please stay away from me please no ahhhhhh!!!"

2.3 • EXTENDING FEEDBACK

Other factors to consider when developing and extending your use of feedback include the following:

2.3.1 • Positive Feedback

Make feedback more positive by explaining why it is being offered and how it might be used constructively.

Many students misunderstand the purpose of feedback, seeing it less as a way to help them learn and improve, and more as a judgment about them and their performance. Keep this in mind when giving feedback and, if necessary, go out of your way to be supportive and positive.

Remember, judgmental or critical comments can undermine a student's motivation and impede learning—whereas we want all students to be empowered and motivated to improve. So in addition to pointing out ways to improve, make sure your feedback encourages and helps keep your students engaged.

▶ Figure 7: Example of Comprehensive Feedback: Teacher's Response

Comprehensive feedback for The Mystery Voice.

I really enjoyed reading this mystery story Alex and you have successfully met the learning intention in the following ways:

1. An excellent opening sentence that makes the reader want to read on!

2. You have included a definite cliff hanger of an ending and I am keen to find out what happens next to Mable.

3. The pace of your story is very good and moves forward while still keeping the reader interested by building up suspense and tension with phrases like 'suddenly the phone rang' and 'her knees were knocking together.'

4. Your choices of adjectives, verbs and adverbs such as: 'nervously,' 'knees knocking,' 'suddenly' and 'deep voice' give your story a scary feel and gives the reader a feeling of urgency and pressure.

To improve your story further:

• You could help the reader to empathize with Mable a bit more and really feel her worry by describing her in more detail: what she looks like, her personality, and so on.

• You could also add more detail to the description of the haunted school. What does it look, feel, smell and sound like? This will help the reader feel even more part of the story and will build on the suspense and tension you have already created.

• Can you identify three other improvements you could make to add to the style and tone of your story?

Well done. I can't wait to read the finished product!

Edward Deci and Richard Ryan identified three situations in which feedback could be counterproductive:

When learners feel too strictly monitored: If learners feel that they are being too closely monitored, they might become nervous or self-conscious and, as a result, disengaged from learning.

When learners interpret feedback as an attempt to control them: Learners may sometimes interpret feedback as an attempt to control them or tell them how they should be doing something rather than as guidance on how to improve.

When learners feel an uncomfortable sense of competition: Feedback shared in a group setting could cause learners to feel that they have to compete with their peers. This can be another source of disengagement in learning.

To avoid these situations, Ryan and Deci (2000b) suggest fully explaining the purpose of any monitoring and ensuring that learners understand that the feedback is meant to help them compete against their own personal bests rather than against each other.

Another effective way to strike the right tone is to communicate your human reaction rather than to adopt an authoritative tone. Also, try to give an *explanation* of what your students have done well so far. Don't just identify the most successful bits but also say *why* those parts are the most successful, identifying the positive effect they are having on the whole outcome.

2.3.2 • Self-Regulation

- -

Self-regulators achieve more. And we're not just talking about the kids involved in Walter Mischel's 1972 marshmallow experiment (see Section 4.1.1)! According to Hattie (2011), students who monitor their own learning have greater confidence to engage further, are more willing to seek and accept feedback and invest more effort into dealing with feedback information.

One way to increase the likelihood that your students will self-regulate is to generate feedback that is ongoing, frequent and an integral part of the learning process. In other words, make sure feedback is not an afterthought added at the end of a piece of work.

Another way is to refrain from giving feedback too early and instead create ample opportunities (and reminders) for students to give themselves and each other feedback. Indeed, this is Step 3 of the Seven Steps to Feedback (see Section 7.1).

Other ways include moving toward getting students to generate their own learning goals and success criteria; reducing the amount of feedback you provide over time; setting up activities in which students give feedback on other students' work, perhaps in groups to begin with and then individually; and giving further instruction after your students have completed their first draft so that they are better able to identify steps they could take to improve their own work.

All of these ideas are explored in more depth in the Seven Steps to Feedback in Chapter 7.

2.3.3 • Tutorials

- -

One of the most effective forms of feedback used by many universities and schools is tutorials. These are generally held in small groups or on a one-to-one basis. Schedule these meetings at regular intervals, and ensure that your students have time to prepare for them. Give those present individualized attention, asking them thought-provoking questions and encouraging them to ask questions themselves.

Tutorials offer an excellent opportunity to offer comprehensive feedback and to set targets for future aspirations and improvements. This is particularly the case if the meeting is generally optimistic and encouraging.

As with all aspects of teaching, this strategy requires good time management. Try meeting with individuals or small groups while other students are working independently. Or meet during break times or after school. The meetings need not last much more than ten to fifteen minutes or so. And of course they do not always need to be led by you; support staff or other colleagues could lead the tutorials.

> Feedback is an important part of self-regulation. And students who are able to self-regulate typically make more progress in their learning.

> Tutorials are an excellent way to give and receive feedback.

2.3.4 • Verbal, Nonverbal or Written

Too many teachers worry that feedback doesn't count unless it is written down. Others spend hours writing in students' books more to impress the school leaders or students' parents than for the sake of the students' learning. This is folly! The quality of feedback should *not* be judged according to what is given but in terms of the benefit it leads to. In other words, leaders and parents should concern themselves with looking for evidence of impact on student learning rather than on whether we teachers have *written* enough feedback.

By taking this attitude, we free ourselves to go back to what we know works best—an environment in which feedback flows in all directions and in all manners: written, verbal, nonverbal, a look, a smile, a nod and a pat on the back.

With all that said, if you still find yourself in an environment that expects formal feedback always to be written, then get your students to write their own feedback (at least some of the time). After tutorials or one-to-one meetings, ask your students to write a record of the advice you have given them. You can even initial this or add to it if you feel the "powers that be" won't accept anything less! In that way, you have a happy medium: you are making sure feedback is generated in dialogue with your students, and at the same time you are giving the record keepers "proof" that feedback has been given. Though why anyone would insist on checking that feedback has been *given* rather than on trying to identify how much has been received, understood and acted upon for the benefit of student learning is anyone's guess!

> The quality of feedback should *not* be judged according to how—or indeed if—the feedback is written down. Instead, it should be judged according to the effect the feedback has on learning.

2.3.5 • Draft-In Recruits

When we were school leaders, we would often volunteer to meet with other teachers' students to give feedback. Imagine how popular this win-win situation was! Students got one-on-one time with another adult; our colleagues felt more supported and part of a team; and we got the opportunity to do some informal moderating that helped identify the consistency of teachers' expectations and variety of judgment calls across the school.

We also found the quality of feedback rose as a result. That is not to brag and say we were the ones who showed exactly how to give great feedback! No, the quality rose because teachers had to be even clearer about the success criteria and "mark scheme" they expected to use when responding to students' learning. This in turn caused all teachers to be clearer with their students about WAGOLL: What A Good One Looks Like.

> When leaders or colleagues offer to give feedback to other people's students, then everyone benefits.

Incidentally, it doesn't have to be the school principal who offers his or her services; other teachers can offer their services too. It might be that the school needs to timetable the opportunities to do this, but it is definitely worthwhile if it can be achieved. Alternatively, support staff, parents or student teachers might be able to offer some degree of support.

2.3.6 • Teach Students to Give Feedback

Asking students to give each other feedback is problematic for many reasons, including these:

- Students don't know what to say.
- They know no more than the person they're giving feedback to and therefore don't feel able to advise.
- They don't want to hurt someone's feelings.

> Teaching students how to give feedback to themselves and each other is not without its problems. But the long-term benefits far outweigh the short-term costs.

- They think if they say something negative about someone else's work, then someone else might be mean back.

- Some students simply don't have an opinion or care enough about someone else's (or indeed their own) work.

We go into this topic in detail in Chapter 7. For now, though, here are some quick suggestions for teaching students how to give feedback:

1. Critique a piece of work together as a whole class.

2. Split your students into small groups, and ask them to work together to critique a piece of work. Each group can then report back to the whole class.

3. Sometimes it is too difficult for novices to critique a single piece of work or single performance; they just don't know where to start. So give your students three pieces of work or get them to watch three different performances. Ask them to compare and contrast each one by comparing them against agreed-upon success criteria. This might need some guidance such as "One of these is excellent, one is good and one is average. I'd like you to work out which is which and why." Or you could ask them to identify which performance was the most exciting (and why), the most energetic, the least convincing, the most thought-provoking and so on.

4. Create an environment in which mistakes and errors are welcomed and examined (see Chapter 3).

2.3.7 • Feedback to You

When reviewing your students' work, consider it an opportunity to receive feedback as well as to give it. Pay particular attention to what they have understood, what misconceptions they are displaying in their work and what aspects of learning are not as secure as you would like them to be. Then use this information to plan the next lesson for these students.

As John Hattie (2009, p. 173) said in his seminal work, *Visible Learning*:

> The mistake I was making was seeing feedback as something teachers provided to students. . . . I discovered that feedback is most powerful when it is from the student to the teacher . . . what students know, what they understand, where they make errors, when they have misconceptions, when they are not engaged—then teaching and learning can be synchronized and powerful.

To make this work, we need to engage in dialogue with our students. See Section 1.2 for a further explanation of "sitting beside" students.

2.3.8 • Three-Way Conferences

A great way to develop your students' self-feedback strategies is to hold regular three-way conferences. These also have the added benefit of giving you—and your students' parents—insight into how much progress individuals think they are making.

(James) This is a blog entry I wrote back in May 2009 describing the three-way conferences used at one of my favorite schools in New Zealand. You can see the original post at www.sustainedsuccess.blogspot.co.uk.

> Once per term, every child at Douglas Park School is encouraged to invite their parents into school for a Learning Conference, during which he or she explains what

Feedback should be thought of as diagnostic for teachers (helping them identify what to teach next) as much as being diagnostic for students (suggesting how to improve).

Parent/ teacher/ student conferences can be a powerful way to gain maximum benefit from feedback.

they've been learning, how much progress they've made and where they intend to go next. (See Learning Conference Guide online at www.challenginglearning.com/media/2391/learning-conference-guide.pdf.)

The rationale behind these conferences is twofold: the first is straight from John Hattie's book on Visible Learning:

> Parents should be educated in the language of schooling so that home and school can share in the expectations and the child does not have to live in two worlds—with little understanding between home and school. Some parents know how to speak the language of schooling and thus provide an advantage for their children during the school years, while others do not know this language, which can be a major barrier to the home contributing to achievement. (Hattie, 2009)

Second of all, as principal Dick Brown explains: "Assess comes from the Latin for 'sitting beside' so our learning conferences give parents the perfect opportunity to 'sit beside' their child; to encourage our students to take personal responsibility for their learning; to develop their communication and organizational skills; to clarify for themselves and their parents their sense of progress and to further enhance the school-home communication and relationships."

2.4 • REVIEW

This chapter is intended as a checklist to give you a snapshot of how well you are doing with feedback so far. It should help to answer the first two of the three key feedback questions: What am I trying to achieve? How much progress have I made so far? What should I do next?

Here are the main points in the checklist:

1. Feedback should be an ongoing part of the learning process, not an added extra at the end of the lesson.

2. All students can benefit from feedback, not just those who are struggling.

3. Feedback needs to be well timed.

4. Effective feedback leads to learners taking actions to improve their performance.

5. Feedback needs to be understood well enough by those receiving it so that they know what to do next.

6. Good feedback begins with criteria that identify What A Good One Looks Like (WAGOLL).

7. Feedback should make reference to the goals that the person is striving for.

8. Error correction is rather like proofreading: it focuses on mechanics such as the accuracy of language and facts. Content critique focuses on the meaning and substance of a performance. The former could—and perhaps should—be left to students' self-reviews, whereas the latter is what we as teachers should focus on.

9. Component feedback is related to individual items, whereas comprehensive feedback looks at the overall performance.

10. Feedback should be positive, supportive and engaging.

11. Teach your students how to give themselves feedback. Then give them time and the expectation to self-regulate.

12. Set up tutorials in which you can give more individualized attention, ask thought-provoking questions and encourage your students to ask you questions.

13. Three-way conferences are a great opportunity for your students to practice giving themselves feedback. They also give you and your students' parents an insight into what individuals are thinking.

14. Feedback does not need to be written! The quality of feedback should be judged according to the benefit it leads to, not in terms of how the message was delivered.

15. If you are a leader, then offer to take some of the feedback workloads off your colleagues. Suggest to your colleagues that you can meet with a handful of their students to give feedback on a current piece of work. This will give you great insight into the quality of learning and feedback in your school and will help ease the pressure on your colleagues. It is a win-win.

16. Teach students how to give feedback so that they do not become over-reliant on you. There is a lot more about this in Chapter 7.

17. When reviewing your students' work, consider it as much an opportunity to receive feedback as to give it. Pay particular attention to what they have understood, what misconceptions they are displaying in their work, and what aspects of learning are not as secure as you would like them to be. Then use this information to plan the next lesson for these students.

2.5 • NEXT STEPS

Here are some suggestions to help you with your reflections on feedback:

1. Out of the seventeen recommendations for high-quality feedback, which ones do you think you are doing very well with so far?

2. Which ones do you think you need to improve on?

3. Based on this short audit, what could you do next to further improve feedback for your students?

4. Of the actions you have thought of in response to the previous question, which one is likely to have the most significant impact on the quality of learning for your students?

5. Why do you think your chosen action will have the biggest impact?

> "Feedback is a free education to excellence. Seek it with sincerity and receive it with grace."
>
> (Houghtailing, 2013)

CREATING A CULTURE FOR FEEDBACK

3.0 • FEEDBACK UTOPIA

Whether "feedback utopia" could ever exist is a matter for debate. But if we were to describe a near-perfect culture for feedback, then it would be something like this:

> For feedback to work brilliantly, the culture needs to be right.

- Feedback is part of a culture of learning that is based on an atmosphere of exuberant discovery.

- Students get more excited about the opportunity to learn from each other than they do from showing off to each other.

- Everybody enjoys success, but there is a sense of disappointment if it comes at the cost of learning. In other words, easy success is only faintly celebrated.

- Feedback is an integral part of the ongoing learning process. It is not seen as a separate activity that takes place after tasks are complete.

- Feedback is a constructive conversation about the learner's progress toward an agreed-upon goal. It includes clear actions and criteria for meeting—or exceeding—the goal.

- All students welcome feedback, based on the belief that it helps them make progress.

- Partway through a learning task, students share their progress with others and ask for recommendations for improvements.

- When students recognize they've made significant mistakes, there is no attempt to hide them. Instead, they invite others to examine those mistakes and suggest solutions.

- Similarly, if a number of students make the same mistake, then the teacher shares the mistake with the whole class so that everyone can engage in analysis and problem solving.

- No one feels ashamed or bashful about making mistakes. There is an assumption that learning leads to mistakes.

- If anyone manages to avoid making mistakes, then it is assumed they must have stayed well within their comfort zone.

- Feedback is generated through dialogue with each other. It is not presented as a monologue from expert to novice.

- Students respond eagerly to feedback and take subsequent action to move closer to—or beyond—their goals.

- Feedback challenges, motivates and supports learners to reach or exceed their goals.

- Everybody gives each other feedback in a collaborative, positive and productive manner.

- Feedback is personalized, well timed and constructive.

- Students have learned how to self-regulate and are reflective at all times. They reaffirm what their goals are, check they are still on course, question whether the process they are using is still fit for purpose and decide what they should do next to move closer to their learning goals.

- Coaching, formative assessment and peer reviews are all used regularly.

- Grading is used sparingly, if at all. When used, grades are viewed as checks against long-term goals.

- Everyone is included in the feedback culture. All students—whether novice or proficient—and all teaching staff give, receive and learn from feedback.

- Teachers, leaders and support staff show that they also enjoy and learn from feedback.

Now, hands up if you have ever witnessed such a utopia! No? OK, but that shouldn't stop us striving *toward* that ideal, should it? If artists can imagine the most stunning image they wish to create, if scientists can search for a perfect cure, if athletes can train for years for just one or two shots at breaking the world record, then surely as teachers we can strive to create a brilliant feedback environment.

Dreaming this and achieving this are two very different things, of course. So here are some essential elements to consider when building *toward* a near-perfect feedback environment.

3.1 • TEN WAYS TO BUILD *TOWARD* FEEDBACK UTOPIA

This section presents some essential elements to consider when building *toward* a near-perfect feedback culture.

3.1.1 • Build Safety and Trust

Safety and trust should be at the heart of feedback. Without these, none—or at least very few—of the characteristics described in Section 3.0 are going to come into being. Or, as Alan E. Beck (1994) put it, "You can't do the Bloom stuff until you take care of the Maslow stuff."

An excellent feedback culture would be built on trust.

Of course, we can't control all of the influences that impinge on a young person's sense of safety and well-being. However, there are many things we can do to use feedback to help build an atmosphere of trust and intellectual safety, including these:

Be Transparent: Ensure feedback relates to clear learning goals. Your students should know what goals for learning they are working toward before they start so that the feedback they receive does not come as an unwelcome surprise.

Be Fair: All students benefit from high-quality, well-timed and productive feedback. Try not to focus your attentions too much on some students at the expense of other students. As mentioned in Section 2.1.2, even the best students need your guidance to improve.

Be Nice: Students learn more from the teachers they like. So be a likable person! Treat students with respect, offer positive reinforcement, smile, listen, show an interest in students' interests and greet each student by name. In other words, show that you care *for* them and *about* them.

Be Consistent: Agree on the learning goals beforehand and then ensure that feedback focuses on these goals. Avoid inconsistencies such as referencing learning goals with some students while offering unrelated feedback to others.

Personalize Feedback: Get to know your students as well as you can. What motivates them? How confident are they? What makes them tick? Once you know answers to these questions, tailor feedback accordingly so that each and every student is encouraged.

. . . Without Being Personal: Feedback should relate to actions rather than to the person. As explored in Sections 1.5 and 2.3.1, feedback that is directed toward the qualities of a person (even if those qualities are positive) can have a negative effect on learning. So always focus feedback on outcomes, actions or ideas.

3.1.2 • Create a Learning Focus

In our many years of working in schools and analyzing research data, we have observed this:

An excellent feedback culture would have a focus on learning and progress.

1. Improved performance comes from a learning focus.

2. Learning does *not* always come from a performance focus.

In other words, if you and your students focus on learning, then their performance grades will also increase. However, if you and your students focus on grades alone, then rich learning opportunities might be missed along the way.

A learning focus includes an emphasis on questioning, challenging, striving to get better and beating personal bests. A performance focus hinges on grades, attainment, showing what you can do and beating each other.

A performance focus *can* lead to academic success, but it may not encourage a critical mind. Students with a performance focus often satisfy themselves with answering questions correctly rather than *also* questioning whether there are better answers—or indeed, better questions. These are the students who ask, "Will I need this for the test?"

A learning focus, on the other hand, is related to mastery. Students with a learning focus go beyond the first answer to seek alternative explanations. They ask questions such as why, if and what about? They see tests as part of the learning process rather than as end points. They seek to make connections, find the significance of parts in relation to the whole and look for ways to transfer ideas to other contexts.

> **When your students have a performance focus, they seek to _prove_ their competence. When they have a learning focus, they seek to _improve_ their competence.**

3.1.3 • Reframe Feedback as Clues for Learning

Too many students—and perhaps too many teachers—believe feedback is a judgment _about them_. This makes feedback that is negative (or feels negative) as unwelcome as a mosquito bite.

> **If we can frame feedback as information to learn from, then the giving and receiving of feedback becomes far less threatening.**

Another way to think about it is to reimagine feedback as the revealing of clues with which to solve a mystery or reach a goal. This makes the whole process much more desirable.

So when you set learning goals with your students, try presenting them as if they are the X marking the spot on a treasure map. Create a sense of desire to reach X by outlining the benefits. Invite clarifying and thought-provoking questions to build your students' appetite for the learning journey. Say you are really looking forward to witnessing the _eureka_ moments (see Section 3.1.4 and Chapter 7) you anticipate will occur as they get closer and closer to X.

Once that's all set up—and of course, that's no mean feat—then it will be much easier to reframe feedback as clues to help students on their learning journey. In such an atmosphere, your students will be champing at the bit to receive the next clue. And if you remind them that it is in everyone's interest to get as many people closer to X as possible, then your students ought to be more enthusiastic about sharing their ideas and strategies (in other words, feedback) with each other.

Of course, this all sounds very idealistic, but if you can move _toward_ this scenario, then imagine the effect it could have on your students' learning! Rather than feedback being viewed as necessary criticism, it could be viewed as a desirable advantage; instead of being avoided unless absolutely necessary, it could be sought out at optimum intervals; and instead of being thought of as a grade in retrospect, it could be thought of as advice to achieve even more.

3.1.4 • Design for Eureka Moments

Students are more likely to seek out and welcome feedback when they are engaged in tasks that lead to a eureka moment. As described in Section 3.1.3, a eureka moment is when a student feels a sense of revelation. It is when they believe they have figured it out for themselves.

An excellent feedback culture would consider feedback to be the revealing of clues for learning.

An excellent feedback culture would include eureka moments. These are when students discover a sense of clarity in their learning.

Coming from the Greek for "I found it," eureka moments are exactly that: "I found it. My teacher didn't give me the answer. My friend didn't show me how to do it. I discovered it for myself. I figured it out and I feel great."

The key to eureka is that the feelings are generated only when students have had to struggle to reach an understanding. If your students do not engage in challenging tasks, then they will have no chance of reaching their eureka moments. If success has come too easily for them, then they may well feel a sense of relief at having "finished," but they will not experience the elation of eureka.

Eureka feels great. So once your students experience eureka, they will want to repeat it again and again. This will lead to an increased willingness to engage in challenging tasks, which in turn will lead to a greater desire for feedback: It is when students are engaged in demanding tasks that they will want more feedback.

Increase the challenge and you will increase your students' desire for feedback!

3.1.5 • Reframe Challenge as More Interesting (Not More Difficult)

Feedback should offer challenge, motivation and support each and every time so that the person receiving it is more able to exceed their learning goals.

Unfortunately, however, a mistake many of us make is to suggest that making things more challenging is the same as making things more difficult. No wonder so many of our students try to avoid challenge where possible. After all, who in the world wants to work *harder*?

It is much more productive to link challenge with making things more *interesting*.

So when you notice a task is too easy for one of your students, say something along the lines of, "Wow, you seem to be finding this easy. Let's make it more interesting by increasing the challenge, shall we?" Definitely do *not* say, "You're finding this easy, so let's make it *harder,* shall we?" Talk about discouraging students from having a go at challenging tasks!

Always associate challenge with being interesting and easy tasks with being boring. By doing this, you will encourage your students to seek out and engage in more challenging tasks, which in turn will increase their desire for feedback.

A good way to plan for this is through the use of the Teaching Target Model (Nottingham, 2010a, 2017).

3.1.6 • Keep Half an Eye on Brain Research

In recent years, there has been an explosion of theories about how people learn. Exciting discoveries in neuroscience and continued developments in cognitive psychology have presented new ways of thinking about the brain. Explanations of how the brain works have used metaphors varying from computers that process information and create, store and manipulate data, to a jungle with its layered world of interwoven, interdependent neurological connections.

However, we should be careful about how we link current research into how the brain works, particularly if we then make recommendations about specific approaches to learning. Scientists caution that the brain is complex, and although research has revealed some significant findings, there is no widespread agreement about their applicability to education.

> An excellent feedback culture would identify challenge as being more interesting and easy tasks as dull and uninteresting.

> An excellent feedback culture would acknowledge what brain research suggests to be true: that challenge is good for students neurologically as well as pedagogically.

That said, there seems to be general agreement about the following:

- **Lessons that are stimulating and challenging are more likely to pass through the reticular activating system (a filter in the lower brain that focuses attention on novel changes perceived in the environment).**

- Experiences that are free of intimidation may help information pass through the amygdala's affective filter.

- When learning is pleasurable, the brain releases dopamine, a neurotransmitter that stimulates the memory centers and promotes the release of acetylcholine, which in turn increases focused attention.

If these early findings are accurate, then perhaps we can also assume that feedback will flourish under similar conditions. That is to say that feedback is improved when it is stimulating, challenging and free from intimidation.

3.1.7 • Walk the Talk

Everyone involved in a learning environment should walk the talk—including the teachers. As the saying goes, "Children are great imitators, so give them something great to imitate."

To be the embodiment of a great feedback culture, we should share these ideas with our students:

- We often make mistakes.

- We believe mistakes are a normal part of learning.

- We don't have all the answers.

- We look to others for support and guidance.

- We welcome feedback as part of our learning journey.

- We examine our mistakes as a way to learn most from them.

- We are always trying to improve the way in which we give, receive and act upon feedback.

3.1.8 • Share the Culture

Feedback should be a constructive conversation about a student's progress toward an agreed-upon goal. It should never be given or perceived as personal criticism.

To increase the likelihood of this becoming a reality, make sure you share with everyone—colleagues, students and parents—what type of feedback culture you are aiming to engender. Engage everyone in creating and promoting the culture. Help them know what they should expect an excellent feedback culture to feel like, sound like and look like.

As part of this, be open to a 360-degree process of feedback. This means inviting, valuing and responding to feedback from colleagues, managers, students and yourself; in other words, from everyone around you—hence the term 360 degrees. This is in contrast to the more common forms of feedback that come from manager to employee or from teacher to student.

Remember that feedback is often influenced by the prevailing learning culture and not just by the relationship between the individuals giving and receiving the feedback. So pay close attention to the learning culture, and ensure you do all you can to build and share the positive aspects of that culture.

An excellent feedback culture would include teachers "walking the talk" and showing that they too welcome and learn from feedback.

An excellent feedback culture would be shared with all members of the school community.

3.1.9 • Keep Feedback Flowing

Feedback should be ongoing, familiar and expected. It should not be something that takes your students by surprise or something that unnerves them. So keep the feedback flowing! And we don't just mean from you to them but also from them to you and from them to each other.

Also remember that feedback is much more effective when it is regular, cumulative and developmental rather than random and unconnected. By being regular, you will enable your students to anticipate and respond to feedback. By being cumulative, feedback will help your students build on their prior learning and make ever more steps toward their learning goals. And by being developmental, feedback will help your students improve and grow their learning abilities.

3.1.10 • Use Feedback to Students as Feedback to You

As mentioned in Section 2.3.7, when you review your students' work, consider it as an opportunity to receive feedback as well as to give it. Pay particular attention to what they have understood, what misconceptions they have and what aspects of learning are less than secure. Then use this information to plan your students' next learning steps.

3.2 • REVIEW

This chapter has covered the following main points:

1. Successful feedback relies on a culture of trust, engagement and exuberant discovery.

2. Students respond best to feedback when it is personalized, well timed and constructive.

3. Feedback is most welcome when it is learning-oriented rather than performance-oriented.

4. Framing feedback as the revealing of clues with which to solve a mystery or reach a goal makes the process more attractive.

5. Increasing your students' desire for challenge will also increase their wish for feedback.

6. Convincing your students that "easy is boring" and "challenging is interesting" helps them be more open to feedback.

7. Early findings from brain research lead us to believe that feedback is improved when it is stimulating, challenging and free from intimidation.

8. Teachers should be seen to positively welcome and act upon feedback. "Walking the talk" is of utmost importance if you want to create the right culture for feedback.

9. Feedback should be a constructive conversation about a student's progress toward an agreed-upon goal. It should never be given, or perceived, as personal criticism.

10. Feedback should be ongoing, familiar and expected. It should not be something that takes your students by surprise or something that unnerves them.

11. Feedback is much more effective when it is regular, cumulative and developmental rather than random and unconnected.

12. The feedback you give your students should inform what you do next to help them in their learning journey. In other words, feedback to them is also feedback to you.

3.3 • NEXT STEPS

Here are some suggestions to help you with your reflections on feedback:

1. Of the ten recommendations for creating a positive culture for feedback, which ones do you have in place so far?

2. Which ones do you think you need to develop?

3. What could you do next to further improve your feedback culture?

4. Of the actions you have thought of in response to the previous question, which one is likely to have the most significant impact on the culture of feedback?

5. Why do you think your chosen action will have the biggest impact?

> "An expert is someone who has succeeded in making decisions and judgments simpler through knowing what to pay attention to and what to ignore."
>
> (De Bono, 2006)

GOALS BEFORE FEEDBACK

4.0 • FEEDBACK SHOULD REFER TO LEARNING GOALS

In the context of education, feedback should be related to the learning journey. Whether it relates to the task, the process or your students' own self-regulation, feedback should always refer to the learning goals.

To illustrate this point, we often ask conference delegates to draw a house. We give everyone forty-five seconds to do so. Why not try it now on the next page?

4.0.1 • Draw a House!

Draw a house here!

Once the forty-five seconds is over, we ask delegates to give each other feedback about their houses.

If you were to give yourself feedback about your house, what would you say? Write your suggestions here.

4.0.2 • Generate Feedback About Your House!

Give yourself some feedback about your house (or ask a friend to give you some feedback).

4.0.3 • Improve Your House!

Now use your feedback to improve your house.

Using the brilliant feedback you've just given yourself, now improve your house! Take no more than twenty seconds to do so. If you have a different-colored pen, use that to make your edits. This will help you track the changes if and when you look back at these pages sometime in the future.

4.0.4 • Review of the House-Drawing Exercise

Looking at the feedback you generated about your house, how useful was it? Did the quality of the finished drawing improve as a result of your feedback? If your feedback was of high quality, then your drawing certainly should have improved.

4. Goals Before Feedback

But we bet your feedback wasn't high quality. And therefore we bet your house did *not* improve as a result of your feedback.

Please don't be offended! We are not saying you *can't* give high-quality feedback. We are simply saying you *couldn't* give high-quality feedback in this *particular* task.

We prevented you from generating high-quality feedback because we gave no other instructions than "draw a house." We did not explain what *kind* of house, nor did we identify the features needed in this particular activity. In some ways, of course, that makes things easier for you: it means you can draw *any* house and be happy with it.

However, it also makes things much harder for you because it stops you from generating useful feedback. Without clear criteria for success, the only way you could have answered the three key feedback questions would have been along the lines of the answers shown in brackets below:

1. What am I trying to achieve? **(I'm drawing a house!)**

2. How much progress have I made so far? **(There's my house.)**

3. What should I do next? **(Finish it.)**

Compare this to a different scenario in which we had set up the task this way instead:

> We'd like you to draw a house. The following features should be included:
>
> - between four and six windows (at least one of which is open)
>
> - a front door
>
> - somewhere to post letters
>
> - a sloping roof
>
> - signs of life

Now think about the feedback you could have given yourself after you'd finished your initial drawing! It would probably have been more like the answers shown in brackets in the following examples:

1. What am I trying to achieve? **(I'm drawing a house with five windows, a front door, a letter box, a sloping roof and some signs of life.)**

2. How much progress have I made so far? **(I've drawn the windows, door, letter box and roof.)**

3. What should I do next? **(I need to add some signs of life. I'm thinking perhaps a cat in the window, a dog kennel in the garden and some kids' toys lying around outside.)**

Compare the difference in quality between the answers in brackets in the first example and the answers in brackets in this second example. *That* is why we recommend clarifying learning goals first and then referencing feedback against those goals. Indeed, we would go as far as to say:

> **If you have not clarified the criteria for success, then do not expect feedback to work very well.**

Of course, the problem is, how often are students set tasks without knowing the criteria for success? And when that happens, is it any wonder they find it difficult to generate high-quality feedback for themselves and for each other?

It was difficult to give yourself useful feedback because the task was not elaborated upon and so the Success Criteria were unclear. All you were told was to draw a house.

Clear Learning Intentions and Success Criteria will help to create useful feedback.

If we asked you to write a letter of application for a job but didn't tell you the job specification or the essential criteria, then how would you know what to write? Or if we said there were television producers next door, now go in and impress them, what would you do? How would you know whether to be friendly or formal, serious or comical?

Moreover, how would you give yourself—or any other applicant—useful feedback if you didn't know what the decision maker was looking for? How on earth could you prepare yourself and give yourself a better chance of success without knowing the criteria for success? It is the same for your students! They need to know what success looks like so that they can make more progress toward their learning goals.

4.0.5 • We Are Not Killing Creativity!

When we use this sort of example at conferences, some people worry about the effect on creativity. They start to wonder whether we are advocating a "painting by numbers" approach to learning. The quick answer to this is: no, we are not trying to kill creativity!

To calm any nerves, here is the way in which we might introduce the task in real life:

> I would like you to draw a house, please. Any shape, any size and any style of architecture. You choose what type of dwelling—be it a giant's castle, a hobbit hole or a two-up, two-down semi by the sea. The features we are looking for today are four to six windows (any shape, any size, any location), a front door (doesn't have to be on the ground floor), somewhere to post letters (doesn't have to be a letterbox in the front door—perhaps it could be a hole in the roof for the giant postman), a sloping roof and some signs of life. These are not the only features of a house, and you certainly would not see them on every house. But they are what we are looking for *today*. And more important, they are the features that I would like you to look for when giving each other feedback after you've all finished draft one.

> Agreeing on the Learning Intentions and Success Criteria before an activity begins does *not* have to reduce creativity. In fact, it can support creativity if introduced shrewdly.

Introducing the task in this way will emphasize to your students that Learning Intentions and Success Criteria should not hamper their imagination or individual flair.

Another way to retain creativity is to engage your students in creating the Success Criteria. For example:

> What features would most houses have? Students might say: roof, walls, place to sleep, eat and so on. As they suggest these, you could ask: Do the rooms always have to have four square walls or could they be round? What about the roof: flat, pointy, grass-covered or something else?

4.0.6 • Rocky Owen

(James) When I was eleven, I moved from primary school to secondary school. It is what most children in the United Kingdom do. The primary school I attended had 200 kids in it, but the secondary school had 2,000, so moving was quite a shock. Two months later, my mother died, and that was an even bigger shock.

My response to all this was to become the class clown; I sought attention by trying to make my friends laugh. Unfortunately, though, it also attracted the unwanted attention of my teachers, who didn't see the funny side and thought I was being mischievous instead. (Teachers never seem to have a sense of humor!) Because of this, my teachers labeled me as a "naughty boy." If ever there was a disruption in class, then I would generally be blamed. And indeed many teachers would send me out of class before lessons began simply so that they didn't have to deal with my "naughtiness."

This continued for two years until a new teacher started at the school: Rocky Owen. I don't know what his first name really was, but we called him Rocky because he used to be a boxer. And I loved Rocky. He was an appalling teacher, but I still loved him because he treated me like everyone else. He didn't send me out of class. He let me stay in class and take part in all the lessons.

Good old Rocky Owen!

Then one day, Rocky organized a field trip to Lindisfarne in Northumberland, which is where the Vikings first landed on Britain's peaceful shores. What a fabulous place. As you walk around, you can almost hear the Vikings still marauding.

The trip to Lindisfarne was the second best day of my school career (the best day was the day I left school). I was hooked on Lindisfarne and hooked on Viking history. That was the day I decided I would be a historian when I grew up and spend my days studying Viking history.

After we had returned to school, Rocky asked us all to write an essay about the Viking invasion of Britain. I'd never been so keen to write an essay in all my life! I put more time and effort into that piece of work than I had ever done before: James Nottingham, the Viking historian, aged 13¾.

When I handed in that essay, I did so with optimism. The grading system back then was pretty similar to what it still is in England—an A, B or C was seen as "good," whereas a D, E or F was seen as "bad"—and until my Viking masterpiece, I'd only ever managed to scrape a D grade. But when I handed in this, the longest essay I'd ever written, I assumed I might get a B or maybe even an A if Rocky was in a good mood when he marked it. And guess what I got . . .

D. Not an A or B as I'd expected but a D, the same as always. And I was devastated. After all that time and effort I'd put in, I'd still only managed to get a D.

You see, my essay was still a complete mess. It was just a longer mess. I still had no idea how to write a clear and thought-provoking essay. All I thought was that I had to write lots and lots, and to do so with a smile on my face.

So with that essay went my dreams of becoming a Viking historian. I stopped trying almost as quickly as I had started trying, and in the end I gave up on history altogether.

4.0.7 • Frank Egan

I was telling the story of Rocky Owen while working with Aranmore Catholic College in Perth, Western Australia, back in March 2012. In the audience that day was Frank Egan, a history teacher with more than thirty years' experience. That night, Frank put together the set of Success Criteria shown in Figure 8 and gave the list to his students the following day, saying, "The more of these you manage to do, the better your next history essay is likely to be."

And thank you, Frank Egan!

These are some of the comments Frank received as a result:

- "I can actually see how to improve; it's obvious."
- "I can see that I don't have enough facts in the paragraphs."
- "So a conclusion is that important?"
- "My intro wasn't anywhere close to what is here."

Also, as Frank wrote in an email to me soon after, "One boy wanted to know why something so simple hadn't been shown before."

▶ Figure 8: Success Criteria for Writing a History Essay

	Not shown	Almost there	Completed	Completed and detailed
Introduction				
4+ sentences				
Proposition stated				
Outline of narrative				
Context of topic				
Body of the essay				
3+ paragraphs				
6+ facts per paragraph				
Interrelationships				
Argument is relevant				
Quote with source given				
Conclusion				
3+ sentences				
Summation				
Proof of proposition				
Literacy				
Spelling accuracy				
Grammar structures				
Use of synonyms				

Imagine if Rocky had given my classmates and me that list. I could have leaned over to the clever girl I always sat next to (my thought being that maybe by osmosis I could become clever) and asked, "Psssst. What does he mean, 'an outline of the narrative'? And how do you state a proposition?"

In other words, I could have taken my newly found enthusiasm and channeled it into something that would have actually helped me improve my essay. As it was, I had no idea how to improve because I didn't know what the Success Criteria were.

4.1 • LONG-TERM AND SHORT-TERM GOALS

The two examples given so far—drawing a house and writing a history essay—are both short-term (or at least, time-specific) goals. But of course there are many long-term goals that might also be brought to mind when talking about feedback.

One example of a long-term goal would be the development of self-control.

4.1.1 • The Long-Term Goal of Developing Self-Control

In 1972, Stanford University psychologist Walter Mischel conducted an experiment to find out when the trait of deferred gratification—the ability to wait for something you want—develops in children. The experiment has been repeated many times since, including in the BBC series *Child of Our Time*.

The original experiment involved more than 600 children between the ages of four and six. Sitting in an empty room, the children were offered a treat of their choice: a cookie, a pretzel or a marshmallow. They were each told they could eat their treat, but if they could wait for fifteen minutes without eating it, then they would get a second one.

We encourage you to watch some of the video clips of similar experiments available online. In them you'll see some children refusing to look at their marshmallow, others peeking at it from behind their hands, one boy licking the plate but not the marshmallow and one even stroking it as if it were a pet!

In all, approximately one-third of the children were able to delay their gratification long enough to be rewarded with a second marshmallow. Of course, the older the child, the more likely they were to succeed, but Mischel also found from follow-up studies that the children who could not wait were more likely to have behavioral problems both at home and school; they had lower exam scores; more often struggled to deal with stressful situations or to pay attention; and found it more difficult to maintain friendships. The children who were able to wait also craved the treat but were able to distract themselves by covering their eyes, playing hide and seek or singing songs. Their desire wasn't dispelled; it was merely forgotten.

Forty years after the first experiment, the researchers tracked down sixty of the original participants and invited them to take part in a new study. They were shown a range of flash cards with faces displaying a range of expressions—happy, neutral or fearful—and asked to press a button every time they saw a fearful face.

This may seem an easy task but, as B. J. Casey, the neuropsychologist who carried out the tests along with Mischel, explains, "A happy face is a social cue that is hard to resist" (Casey et al., 2011). The results showed that the participants who had struggled to defer gratification when they were younger also struggled to resist pressing the button when they saw a happy face.

The experiment concluded with many of the participants repeating the test while lying in a brain scanner. The participants with better self-control showed more activity in the part of the brain associated with risk aversion, whereas those with poorer self-control showed increased activity in the brain region associated with reward and addiction.

The lesson of this study is that students should be helped to develop the capacity for waiting and deferring gratification. And, of course, goal setting and feedback can help with this.

> Learning Intentions and Success Criteria shouldn't be used only for short-term goals but also for lifelong learning goals.

> . . . such as learning how to defer gratification and exercise self-control.

> Walter Mischel found that students who develop self-control have more success at school.

4.1.2 • Other Long-Term Goals

Other long-term goals might include helping your students be

Other long-term goals that would benefit from Learning Intentions and Success Criteria include becoming more open-minded, learning how to take intellectual risks and developing resilience and determination.

- curious
- focused on what is relevant
- full of wonder
- keen to learn from mistakes
- open to new experiences
- persistent
- resilient
- risk takers
- self-regulating
- willing to ask for support and coaching

Of course, this is not a hierarchy or an exhaustive list. But setting these or similar attitudes as long-term goals will enable you to tailor feedback to your students accordingly.

It's also worth bearing in mind that Lev Vygotsky, one of the pioneers of educational psychology, wrote at length about learning through culture. By that he meant that young people learn from those around them: what to laugh at, what to be afraid of, what to have a go at, what to avoid and so on. He emphasized that young people pick up mental as well as physical habits from their elders and warned us that the way we react to things is arguably more influential on young minds than the knowledge we share.

That's one heck of a responsibility for those of us who work with young people! It also makes getting feedback right even more essential.

4.2 • LEARNING INTENTIONS (LI) AND SUCCESS CRITERIA (SC)

Being clear about Learning Intentions and Success Criteria will help your students generate their own feedback. It will help you keep your feedback goal-referenced (Section 2.1.8) and consequential (Section 2.1.4). And it will help everyone maintain a learning focus (Section 3.1.2).

Here are definitions of Learning Intentions and Success Criteria:

Learning Intentions describe what students should know, understand or be able to do by the end of the lesson or series of lessons.

Success Criteria list what students should demonstrate to show they have accomplished the Learning Intention. They specify the main things to do, include or focus on.

Together, the Learning Intentions and Success Criteria should help your students answer the three feedback questions:

1. What am I trying to achieve?
2. How much progress have I made so far?
3. What should I do next?

Here are some of the benefits of effective LI and SC—they will

- **help you design effective learning activities for your students**

- **give your students an understanding of what they are aiming to achieve (LI) and what they can do to reach their goal (SC)**

- **provide a scaffold to support your students' progress**

- **offer your students a language with which to articulate their learning**

- **help your students be more self-motivated and independent**

- **give you a focus for asking learning questions and setting supplementary tasks**

- **give students clear reference points for their feedback to each other and to themselves**

- **increase self-regulation**

- **support effective learning reviews**

Very often LI and SC help to improve progress and feedback. However, in some classrooms they are either very poorly used or overused to the point that they are no longer noticed by students.

To help you avoid these pitfalls, the following sections offer some recommendations for making the best use of LI and SC. Many of the recommendations refer to the example LI and SC recently spotted in a classroom for ten- and eleven-year-olds in Newcastle (North East England).

Learning Intention

To understand the differences between England, Great Britain, the United Kingdom and the British Isles.

Success Criteria

- Identify which countries are part of Great Britain, which are part of the United Kingdom and which are part of the British Isles.

- Locate each country on a map.

- Give the full name for the United Kingdom.

4.2.1 • Make LI and SC Relevant

Most students want to know what's in it for them. Why should they learn what you're asking them to learn? What is the point? That is why we should always think about broadcasting in Wii-FM radio: **W**hat's **I**n **I**t **F**or **M**e.

Looking at the map example given, would your students even be interested in knowing the difference between England, Great Britain, the United Kingdom and the British Isles? If not, then how can you increase their motivation for the topic?

In the Newcastle school mentioned, many of the kids loved sports. So the Success Criteria could've been amended like this:

- Identify which five teams make up the British and Irish Lions rugby team.

- Show on a map where each home nation plays its international schedule.

> Learning Intentions and Success Criteria should be designed so as to help students answer the question: What's In It For Me? (Wii-FM).

- Compare the differences between the passports held by the England captain and Irish captain.

Other children in the same class were more interested in music, so the Success Criteria could have been achieved with the following music-themed activities:

- Adele is from England, Tom Jones is from Wales, Ronan Keating is from Ireland, the band Snow Patrol is from Northern Ireland and the band Franz Ferdinand is from Scotland. For each act, explain which region(s) they come from (e.g., Ronan Keating is not British because Ireland is not part of Great Britain).

- Place a photo of each singer/group on the map to show which country they come from. Color-code the cards to show whether that also makes them part of the United Kingdom, Great Britain and/or the British Isles.

- Adele has a UK passport. What does the abbreviation "UK" stand for?

4.2.2 • Co-Create LI and SC

In so far as possible, involve your students in creating the Learning Intentions and Success Criteria. Here are some effective ways to do this:

- Build LI and SC around questions your students have asked during other learning activities.

- Use a stimulus to prompt your students to ask questions, and then use their questions to design LI and SC.

- Preview new subject matter by asking your students what they would *like* to know and what they think they will *need* to know in order to master the new theme.

- Share completed work from other students, and ask your current students to identify what they think the LI and SC were that led to their successful completion.

- Share the LI and then ask your students to suggest what they would need to do to reach that goal (in other words, ask them what the SC should be).

- Share the LI and one or two example SC, then ask your students to suggest other SC.

- Look back at LI and SC your students have used in the past, and ask how accurate and effective they were. Then take the conclusions from that review and apply them in designing new LI and SC for the current topic.

- Offer a long list of SC, and ask your students to identify, or vote for, which criteria they think will be the most effective/interesting/productive.

- Start with a basic set of SC, and ask your students to identify ways to make them more interesting (e.g., the sports-mad kids might suggest that they look through the "lens" of sports, whereas the music-mad kids might ask to base their learning in the context of singer-songwriters from England, Great Britain, the United Kingdom and so on).

> Students will engage more in Learning Intentions and Success Criteria when they take part in creating them.

4.2.3 • Unshackle the Criteria

Giving your students a set of closely defined success criteria can seem a bit like "painting by numbers": do this, this and this, and then you will succeed! As we explore in Chapter 5, this isn't necessarily a bad thing. But it can be a bad thing if it is the only approach you take.

To ensure that there is some variety in the LI and SC your students use, try some of the following suggestions.

A. Include a "So What?" Question

For example:

> SC: Show why it is important to know the difference between England, Great Britain, the United Kingdom and the British Isles.

Or change the LI so that it becomes:

> To determine why anyone would worry what the difference is between England, Great Britain, the United Kingdom and the British Isles.

B. Use LI and SC That Are Open-Ended

Using LI and SC that encourage multiple ways to respond can increase your students' level of interest. Below are a few examples.

Odd One Out

"England, Great Britain, the United Kingdom and the British Isles: Which is the odd one out and why?" Note: You can find out more about the Odd One Out strategy in Chapter 9 of *Challenging Learning Through Dialogue* (Nottingham, Nottingham & Renton, 2017).

Fermi Questions

Create a Fermi question (see *Challenging Learning Through Questioning,* Nottingham & Renton, in press). For example: "How many professional athletes are there in each of England, Great Britain, the United Kingdom and the British Isles?"

Focus on Process

Set up an activity that requires your students to question the process as well as engage in the content. For example: "Out of England, Great Britain, the United Kingdom and the British Isles, decide which is best and say why." To achieve this SC, your students will need to determine what is meant by "best"—for example, best place to go on holiday, best economy, best sports, best music, best place to be a young person and so on.

4.2.4 • Break the Formula

It is a mistake to think that every lesson should begin with a full set of LI and SC. That can lead to very formulaic and predictable lesson introductions (though of course this might not be a bad thing, depending on the age, aptitude and specific needs of your students).

Generally, though, it is a good idea to vary the way in which lessons begin. So when it comes to LI and SC, it might sometimes be more appropriate to start with an open question that leads to exploration rather than start with a predetermined path that LI and SC tend to describe. Or you could have an open beginning and then identify the LI and SC when your students are more familiar with the subject matter.

> Learning Intentions and Success Criteria that have an element of discovery and are open-ended will generally be more attractive to students.

> Including an element of metacognition in the Learning Intentions and Success Criteria will also make them more appealing.

> Remember that lessons do *not* always have to start with Learning Intentions and Success Criteria.

Following are some suggestions for ways in which to vary the timing and use of LI and SC.

A. Stimulus First, LI and SC Second

Begin with a stimulus (e.g., image, story or drama). Draw out the key concepts, then ask your students to select the "best" one (this might require some SC for identifying the "best"). From there, you could invite your students to create some questions worth exploring. Once your students are immersed in this activity, you could then ask them to identify the learning that is taking place and to set targets for the end of the lesson or topic.

For example:

> LI: To understand the difference between nationality and identity
>
> SC: (1) Identify the nationalities of Adele, Tom Jones, Ronan Keating, Snow Patrol and Franz Ferdinand. (2) Suggest why Adele is more likely to say she is British than the members of Franz Ferdinand are. (3) Create a Venn diagram to show the difference between nationality and identity.

B. LI and SC in Review

Immerse your students in an exciting, all-consuming activity without any preamble or goal setting. Then when they start to tire or drift off task, ask them to reflect on what they have been doing and to generate the LI and SC in the review.

C. Steer Clear of Content-Driven LI and SC

As you can see from the house-drawing and essay-writing examples in Section 4.0, it is often very effective to give LI and SC that connect clearly to the mastery of content and skills. However, some students will see this as a preordained path from which they should not veer (though you can limit the frequency of this response by following the advice given in Chapter 5).

If you mix in some LI and SC that are process-driven, then you can prevent your students from approaching the lesson as if it were a tick-box exercise.

For example:

> LI: To collaborate effectively together to identify what we want to know about the different countries of the British Isles
>
> SC: (1) In groups, each individual should share at least one thing that interests them about the topic. (2) As a group, sort the questions you have created (e.g., open/closed, easy to answer/difficult to answer, interesting/dull). (3) As a group, plan your learning and identify the steps you will need to take to achieve the Learning Intention.

Making sure that some Learning Intentions and Success Criteria include a focus on something other than content (e.g., skills or attitudes) will make them more appealing to students.

4.2.5 • Customize and Adapt

Returning to the story of the history essay criteria created by Frank Egan (Section 4.0.7), what Frank found was that all of his students benefited initially. However, after a while it became apparent that some students had outgrown the original list, whereas others were still struggling to understand every aspect of it. So this is where matching different goals to different students became the key.

There are, of course, many ways to personalize LI and SC to suit your students. Here are just a few examples:

- Give some students a long list of criteria and others a shorter list.

- Add some extension tasks to the SC for your more advanced students. (There are lots of examples in the sample SC in Sections 4.4 and 4.5.)

- Differentiate by outcome; that is to say, give all your students the same list of SC but expect the quality and quantity of responses to differ, perhaps considerably (though, of course, don't let your expectations of difference negatively affect how your students respond to the tasks).

- Give a full list of SC to some students, a half list to others for them to complete and ask the most advanced to create their own set of SC.

Learning Intentions and Success Criteria should be individualized as much as possible.

With all these examples, it is worth noting that they are focused on engaging and challenging every student at their level. They should not be used as a way of labeling or grouping according to levels of ability that are presumed (or perceived) to be static. It is our task as educators to take our students beyond their current levels of competence, so the LI and SC we ask our students to engage with should always be just beyond what they can do now. In other words, the LI and SC should take them into their "wobble zone." See *Challenging Learning* (Nottingham, 2016, pp. 52–76) for more about "making students wobble."

4.2.6 • Preview

Previewing a topic before it is due to start is a very effective way to engage your students and increase their learning. Indeed, John Hattie (2009) identified some studies in his database that show previewing topics can have an effect size of 0.9. This compares very favorably with the typical outcome of all effects found in the 65,000 studies that Hattie has analyzed so far, which is an effect size of 0.4. In other words, previewing a topic can help your students make more than double the usual amount of progress!

In this context, previewing means looking ahead to see what is coming next so that your students are better able to prepare for their learning.

Previewing (looking ahead to see what will be studied in the next lesson) can have a significantly positive effect on learning.

When we were teaching full time, we would devote a small amount of time every week to previewing the topics that would be covered the following week. For example, if we were going to begin a new topic on tourism, we would ask our students (a) what they *wanted* to know about tourism and (b) what they thought we *should* know about tourism by the end of the unit. We would then list the questions on the board, group them into units of work (or lesson plans) and, if there was time, begin some initial research. Of course, then some of our students would do some preliminary research over the weekend to prepare for the following week. For others, we would set up preview clubs (much the same as after-school sports or art clubs but with a focus on previewing lessons), and for others still, we would contact the students' parents to encourage them to support their child's learning. You can read more about previewing and the way to support *all* students in *Challenging Learning* (Nottingham, 2016, pp. 42–44).

Of the many benefits to previewing, we found the following to be particularly relevant:

> **Previewing motivates students because they feel more involved in the planning and decision making about their learning.**
>
> **Previewing gives students the opportunity to prepare better for lessons. Too often, students do not know what's coming up until the moment the lesson begins, whereas previewing allows thinking time, opportunities to do some preparatory research and the possibility of approaching lessons in a prepared state of mind.**
>
> **Previewing can allow parents to support their children's learning more effectively. So, rather than feeling disconnected from their child's schooling, parents are given the opportunity to engage more in their child's studies.**
>
> **Previewing can be particularly effective for students who are finding it difficult to keep up with their classmates. Giving these students a "heads-up" on what is coming next generates a sense of confidence as well as a head start. This in itself makes previewing—even with just a small group—worthwhile.**

Taking all this into account, it appears that one of the best times to share LI and SC is as part of a preview activity. Of course, this might not always be appropriate, but when it is then it is definitely recommended—even if that is just for those students you know need a little boost to catch up.

4.2.7 • Make LI and SC Worthwhile!

There is very little point in spending time and effort preparing excellent LI and SC if you don't then refer to them during the lessons! The whole point of them is to give your students a clear set of expectations for the lesson and to help them give feedback to themselves and each other. However, if LI and SC become merely a routine for the beginning of lessons (as we have seen time and again in classrooms in the United Kingdom), then they will lose their very potency.

So once you have set, created or agreed on the LI and SC, then ensure that you make good use of them in the following ways:

Using LI and SC to Generate Questions

Make the LI and SC the focus for your supplementary questioning.

For example:

- What have you found out about the British and Irish Lions so far?
- How many of you have discovered the difference between Great Britain and the United Kingdom so far?
- Who could give me a suggestion as to why our Learning Intention is important to a lot of people?
- Which of the singers we identified belongs to the most number of categories between English, British, UK citizen and part of the British Isles?

Learning Intentions and Success Criteria should be referred to throughout the learning process, not just at the beginning and end.

Learning Intentions and Success Criteria should be used to generate relevant and thought-provoking questions.

Using SC to Identify How Much Progress Individuals Have Made

Use the SC to ascertain how much progress individual students have made so that you can decide whether to offer more support or more challenge.

For example:

> Here is a possible supporting question: The British and Irish Lions are made up of rugby players from five countries. I think you've identified three of those countries so far. Can you find the other two?

> Here is a possible challenging question: If Scotland had voted for independence in 2014, how do you think that would have affected England, Great Britain, the United Kingdom and the British Isles?

Using LI and SC to Review Learning

When you prompt your students to review their learning, then of course the LI and SC should feature prominently in their thinking.

Here are some example questions:

- How much progress do you think you've made toward our Learning Intention?

- Which SC did you find easy to achieve? Which ones were more challenging?

- What strategies for learning did you use to make progress toward our learning goal?

- What was the most interesting thing you found out about the differences between England, Great Britain, the United Kingdom and the British Isles?

- What questions do you have now that you would like us all to try to answer next time?

4.2.8 • Use SC to Generate Feedback

This might not be "saving the best 'til last," but it is most definitely saving the most important until last. If the SC are not used as a focal point for feedback, then we really are missing a trick! That's why this chapter about LI and SC is the most comprehensive in the whole book. Learning Intentions help to answer the first feedback question; the Success Criteria should help your students answer the other two questions:

1. What am I trying to achieve?

2. How much progress have I made so far?

3. What should I do next?

As we showed with the house-drawing exercise (see Section 4.0), suitable Success Criteria can mean the difference between good feedback and bad. Or, in fact, between good feedback and no feedback at all.

So make sure your students always relate their feedback to the Learning Intentions and Success Criteria!

> Learning Intentions and Success Criteria can help students identify how much progress they have made so far and what their next steps could be.

> Learning Intentions and Success Criteria can give students the right language and focus with which to review their own learning journey.

> Learning Intentions and Success Criteria are there to improve the quality of feedback!

4.3 • HOW TO DESIGN EFFECTIVE LI AND SC

> **Remember that Learning Intentions and Success Criteria should always be**
>
> - **understood by your students**
> - **matched to each individual's needs**
> - **connected to big, worthwhile ideas**
> - **meaningful to your students' lives**

This section presents a guide to designing the most effective Learning Intentions and Success Criteria.

4.3.1 • Know, Understand and Be Able To

Designing effective Learning Intentions should start with these questions:

- What do I want students to know?
- What do I want students to understand?
- What do I want students to be able to do?

It can be problematic to answer these questions *and* put them into language that is meaningful to your students. However, time spent on this preliminary step is in itself excellent professional learning. Indeed, some schools make this the focus of planning days. The result, they claim, is that staff have a better understanding of the curriculum and increased confidence in the consistency of approach across the school.

Knowledge

Being specific about the kinds of knowledge you want your students to gain should help you design productive and varied Learning Intentions.

For example, you could consider:

- knowledge *about* a particular topic (e.g., know about the difference between Great Britain, the United Kingdom and the British Isles)
- knowledge of *how* something is done (e.g., know how to read a map to show where Great Britain, the United Kingdom and the British Isles are)
- knowledge of *why* something is important (e.g., know why it is important to be able to distinguish between Great Britain, the United Kingdom and the British Isles)
- knowledge of *what* causes something (know what caused the creation of the different regions)

Understanding

Understanding builds on knowledge and requires some form of intellectual processing.

Learning Intentions and Success Criteria should identify what students should know . . .

. . . what they need to understand . . .

For example, your students might be able to list the causes of a historical event (thereby showing knowledge of them), but for them to *understand* the causes will require analysis and interpretation.

This makes understanding more demanding than knowledge. So when you design Learning Intentions, try to create a balance of knowledge and understanding so there is an opportunity for all of your students to engage.

These are some examples of Learning Intentions focused on understanding:

- Understand the *causes* of a historical event.

- Understand the *effects* of diet on health.

- Understand how *persuasive* language can encourage readers to agree with the author.

- Understand how the Web can be used for *research* purposes.

- Understand *what happens* when our bodies consume carbohydrates.

- Understand why X *causes* Y.

- Understand the *significance* of symbolism in religion.

Skills

Learning Intentions that focus on skills always begin with the words *to be able to* followed by a verb.

For example:

- To be able to *write* a recount or report of something that happened

- To be able to *solve* a problem using more than one strategy

- To be able to *work* as part of a team

- To be able to *identify* persuasive strategies used by the author or an argument

- To be able to *experiment* with a variety of media in order to achieve a stated effect

Often, Learning Intentions that focus on skills also imply the acquisition of certain knowledge or understanding. For example, to be able to write a recount or report of something that happened, students would need knowledge of the structures and features of a report.

4.3.2 • Write Learning Intentions

Here are some ways to improve the style and quality of Learning Intentions.

A. Set the Learning Intention in Context

- Link the Learning Intention to the bigger picture (e.g., to help us divide numbers, we are learning how to use a number line)

- And/or connect the Learning Intention to prior learning (e.g., after using a number line to count in twos, now we are learning to use a number line to divide by 3)

- Link the learning to the long-term aims for your students (e.g., we are developing our numeracy skills by learning how to use a number line to divide by 3)

> . . . and what they could do to reach their learning goal.

> Learning Intentions are more relevant if they include clear links with past and future learning.

B. Use SMART Learning Intentions

SMART is a mnemonic acronym that sets out criteria for achieving goals, particularly in the workplace. The S normally stands for Specific; the M generally stands for Measurable. The other letters have different meanings for different authors. For us in this context, SMART means this:

Specific: LI should be clearly defined and concise.

Measurable: LI should have aspects that can be measured so that your students have a sense of how much progress they've made so far.

Achievable or Aspirational: Depending on your purpose, LI should be challenging enough to engage your students but realistic enough to give them some chance of success, that is, Achievable. Other times, LI should instead be Aspirational so that they help your students aim higher than they ever thought was possible.

Relevant: LI must be relevant to your students' current stage of learning so that they build on past knowledge, skills and understanding and build toward further exploration and engagement.

Timely: LI should be timed just right so that they capture the interest of your students. For example, they should be connected to a hot topic, current affairs, an issue that has been circulating around school recently or questions that your students have asked spontaneously as part of some other learning.

C. Use Child-Friendly Language

- Keep the Learning Intention clear and meaningful in language that is appropriate for the age and stage of your students.

- Increase your use of technical terms as your students become more able to understand and deal with them.

D. Use Words Associated With Learning

- Clear Learning Intentions should help your students focus not just on the tasks but also on their learning. They should also give your students a language for learning. It might help to begin with phrases such as these:

    We are learning to . . .

    We are aiming to understand that/how . . .

    We are (challenging our) thinking about . . .

    We are learning how to be able to . . .

Here is some learning language we use in the example Learning Intentions in Section 4.4:

1. Learn how to
2. Identify and name
3. Write and create
4. Plan and produce
5. Sort and point out
6. Understand meaning and significance; know about
7. Recognize and relate
8. Develop, engage and understand how to
9. Experiment with
10. Examine
11. Compose
12. Compare
13. Use and interpret
14. Value and respect
15. Understand significance
16. Make sense of, interpret and recognize
17. Understand why
18. Find out about

Here is some learning language we use in the example Learning Intentions in Section 4.5:

1. Understand how
2. Develop awareness
3. Understand what
4. Explain significance
5. Learn about and identify how
6. Apply and adapt
7. Produce
8. Broaden
9. Recognize
10. Identify differences, causes and consequences
11. Define

You will also find inspiration for the sorts of learning words you might use by looking at our analysis of Bloom's taxonomy in Section 5.2.

Make sure
that students
can refer to
the Learning
Intentions
throughout
the learning
process.

E. Display the Learning Intention

- Display the Learning Intention(s). They can provide a reference point for your students throughout the learning process—and be a particularly useful guide when your students generate feedback for themselves and each other.

4.3.3 • Design Effective Success Criteria

Here are some ways to improve the style and quality of Success Criteria:

A. Link the Success Criteria to the Learning Intention

- Success Criteria should summarize the key steps or ingredients your students will need to achieve the Learning Intention.

- The criteria should always flow from the Learning Intention and include the main things to do, include or focus upon.

- Keep the focus more on the learning than on the doing.

Success Criteria
should show the
steps needed
to achieve
the Learning
Intention.

B. Create a Balance of Success Criteria

- Vary the focus for Success Criteria so that over a week or two, you have used words that emphasize learning, knowledge, understanding, thinking strategies and skills (see Sections 5.2 and 5.3 for inspiration).

- Make sure some Success Criteria are process-driven. Indeed, this would be the case more often than not in math. For example:

When viewed
together,
multiple sets
of Success
Criteria should
include a
broad range of
attitudes, skills
and knowledge.

Learning Intention

To multiply two-digit numbers using partitioning

Success Criteria

    i. Write down the multiplication number sentence.

    ii. Partition the biggest number into tens and units.

    iii. Multiply each partitioned number by the multiple.

    iv. Add the answers together to the find the overall answer.

    v. Complete the number sentence.

Worked Example

    i. $35 \times 3 =$

    ii. 35 into 30 and 5

    iii. $30 \times 3 = 90, 5 \times 3 = 15$

    iv. $90 + 15 = 105$

    v. $35 \times 3 = 105$

C. Model Success

- Your students need a good idea of what a successful outcome is like.

- You can share the standard you are expecting by using examples linked to the Success Criteria. For example, you could show three pieces of work, describing one as average, one as good and one as excellent. Remember to make the link between the Success Criteria and your judgment of each piece of work.

- This works equally well with performance-based learning. You could show video clips or invite live performances of varying degrees of success. Again, remember to link your judgment clearly to the Success Criteria.

Success Criteria can be brought to life through the sharing of WAGOLL (What A Good One Looks Like) examples.

D. Involve Your Students in Creating Success Criteria

- Involve your students in the process of identifying Success Criteria by asking them what actions would need to be taken in order to reach the learning goal.

- Share two or three completed examples of varying quality, and ask your students to identify the Success Criteria that could've been used to make judgments about quality.

- Provide the first two or three Success Criteria and then ask your students for suggestions about additional criteria.

Sometimes it works best to share WAGOLL first and then ask students to create the Success Criteria.

E. Personalize Success Criteria

- One size does not fit all! Ideally, your LI and SC will be individualized to accommodate the varying stages of development of your students.

- The LI and SC should also be personalized to suit students whose barrier to learning is attitudinal. You could do this by including aspects of the ASK model (see Section 5.4.4).

- Use effective questioning techniques to more closely identify what individual students need in terms of support and challenge.

- Teach your students how to generate their own Success Criteria so that they can independently create their own set.

- Use tools such as the Learning Challenge (see Section 6.1 and Chapter 8) to help students clarify where they are in their learning journey and which Success Criteria would help them next.

As with Learning Intentions, the best Success Criteria are tailor-made to match individuals' learning needs.

4.4 • EXAMPLE LI AND SC TO USE WITH FIVE- TO ELEVEN-YEAR-OLDS

This section presents some examples of LI and SC we have used recently with students. Seeing age as stage of development is arguably more important than chronological age, we have given an age range purely as a loose guide.

The underlined words show the main learning language verbs (see Section 4.3.2D) we have used.

The *bullet points in italics* are suggestions for extension criteria (see Section 4.2.5).

The underlined words identify the learning language that can be used to teach students how to learn (as well as what to learn).

4.4.1 • Math: Division

Six- to eight-year-olds

Learning Intention

To <u>learn how</u> to use a number line to divide whole numbers

Success Criteria

To reach our learning goal, we will be able to:

- <u>Start</u> from 0 and jump in steps according to the number we are dividing by (e.g., jump three steps when dividing by 3).

- <u>Stop</u> jumping when we reach the big number we are dividing into.

- <u>Count</u> how many jumps we made to get there.

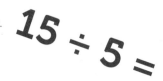

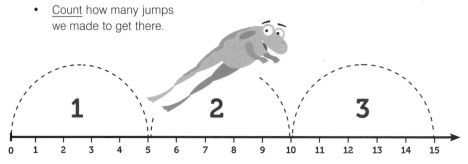

4.4.2 • Math: Equivalent Fractions

Seven- to eight-year-olds

Learning Intention

To <u>identify and name</u> equivalent fractions; for example, ½ (half) is the same as ¾ (two quarters)

Success Criteria

To reach our learning goal, we will be able to:

- <u>Use</u> objects or drawings to show equivalent fractions.

- <u>Show</u> examples of equivalent fractions in number form.

- <u>Write</u> a story using equivalent fractions.

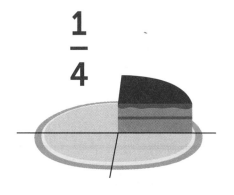

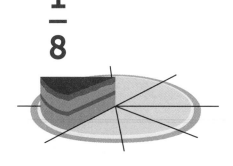

4.4.3 • Literacy: Scary Story

Eight- to ten-year-olds

Learning Intention

To write a mystery story that uses descriptive words to <u>create</u> a scary atmosphere

Success Criteria

To reach our learning goal, we will be able to:

- <u>Set</u> the scene in the opening paragraph.
- <u>Build</u> up tension/suspense.
- <u>Use</u> spooky adjectives and powerful verbs.
- <u>End</u> with a cliffhanger.
- *Decide which five words you've used are the most effective at creating a scary atmosphere.*

4.4.4 • Literacy: Report Writing

Nine- to eleven-year-olds

Learning Intention

To <u>plan and produce</u> a piece of writing that accurately orders and describes a series of events

Success Criteria

To reach our learning goal, we will be able to:

- <u>Recognize</u> key features and the structure of report writing by examining other texts (e.g., diaries, newspaper articles, personal stories).
- Use a fortune line (see www.challenginglearning.com) to <u>chart</u> the chronology and personal impact of events in the piece.
- <u>Write</u> in the first or third person.
- <u>Make good use</u> of the past tense.
- <u>Understand</u> the function of and accurately use time connectives in our writing.
- <u>Focus</u> on specific people or events rather than general topics.
- *Discuss with your partner whether future events could ever be included in a piece of report writing.*

4.4.5 • Science: Materials and Their Properties

Seven- to nine-year-olds

Learning Intention

To <u>sort</u> between solids and liquids and to <u>point out</u> examples of liquids that are not water

Success Criteria

To reach our learning goal, we will be able to:

- Correctly <u>sort</u> materials (e.g., wood, iron, shampoo, shaving foam) as liquid or solid using a Venn diagram.

- <u>Describe similarities</u> between solids and liquids (e.g., solids and liquids can be measured).

- <u>Describe differences</u> between solids and liquids (e.g., you can pour liquids but not solids).

- <u>Classify</u> items such as sponge, rice and sand.

- *<u>Determine</u> what something is called if it is neither a solid nor a liquid.*

4.4.6 • History: Settlement

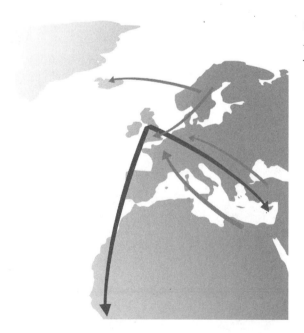

Nine- to eleven-year-olds

Learning Intention

To <u>recognize</u> that people have been moving between different areas throughout history and for different reasons, and to <u>relate</u> these movements to modern-day journeys

Success Criteria

To reach our learning goal, we will be able to:

- <u>Locate</u> places on a map to show journeys people you know have taken.

- <u>Discuss and relate</u> our own experiences of moving home.

- <u>Summarize</u> the different reasons why people might move.

- <u>Outline</u> the journeys made by some of the groups we have studied in the past (e.g., Romans and Vikings).

- <u>Distinguish between</u> words such as *settlement, emigration, immigration* and *refugee* and how these are different from words like *invasion* and *conquest*.

- *<u>Imagine and describe</u> how you would feel if you had to move from one country to another. Say how this would be different from choosing to travel.*

4.4.7 • Physical Education: Hockey

Seven- to nine-year-olds

Learning Intention

To <u>develop control</u> of the ball when dribbling in hockey; to <u>engage</u> in cooperative physical activity; to <u>understand how</u> to play in a safe way

Success Criteria

To reach our learning goal, we will be able to:

- <u>Hold</u> the stick in two hands at all times.
- Use the stick to <u>maintain</u> control of the ball.
- Keep our head up to <u>avoid</u> collisions with other people.
- <u>Change</u> direction to move between markers.
- <u>Stay safe</u> by using the equipment correctly.
- *Suggest which drills would be the best for improving our technique.*

4.4.8 • ICT: Creating Pictures

Six- to eight-year-olds

Learning Intention

To <u>experiment</u> with information communication technology (ICT) in order to create pictures

Success Criteria

To reach our learning goal, we will be able to:

- <u>Identify how</u> ICT can be used to create pictures.
- <u>Select</u> appropriate tools to create pictures that communicate ideas (e.g., control the pen and use the "flood fill" tool to create visual affects; use the "straight line, geometric shapes" and "flood fill" tools to match their purposes; use the "spray" tool).
- <u>Choose</u> colors and patterns to match their purposes.
- <u>Show</u> that you can store your work using the "save as" command.
- *Suggest how ICT has helped you and how it has hindered you in this lesson.*

4.4.9 • Art: Visual Interpretation

Ten- to twelve-year-olds

Learning Intention

To <u>examine</u> the differences between a photograph and a drawing of the same image

Success Criteria

To reach our learning goal, we will be able to:

- <u>Identify</u> similarities and differences between the drawing and the photograph.
- <u>Predict</u> which medium is best for different purposes.
- <u>Explore</u> the crossover between photographs and drawings.
- *<u>Propose</u> which is the best way to record real life and say why.*

4.4.10 • Music: Composing

Eight- to ten-year-olds

Learning Intention

To <u>compose</u> simple rhythms and melodies

Success Criteria

To reach our learning goal, we will be able to:

- <u>Identify the value</u> of notes regarding their time value.
- <u>Know what</u> a half note and eighth note represent in the music world.
- <u>Recognize</u> the symbol for rest.
- <u>Play</u> a simple written rhythm.
- *In pairs, <u>combine</u> compositions to form a new composition.*

4.4.11 • Geography: A Village in India

Seven- to nine-year-olds

Learning Intention

To use maps to compare the difference between two localities

Success Criteria

To reach our learning goal, we will be able to:

- Locate the United Kingdom and India.

- Draw a local map of the United Kingdom and one of Chembakolli showing an awareness of main human and physical features in both localities.

- Prepare a simple route map and commentary to show a route to India.

- Describe what we think Chembakolli village is like.

- *Guess the type of person who would prefer to live in Chembakolli and the type of person who would like to live in the United Kingdom.*

4.4.12 • Geography: Maps and Scales

Ten- to eleven-year-olds

Learning Intention

To use and interpret maps drawn with a variety of scales

Success Criteria

To reach our learning goal, we will be able to:

- Compare the similarities and differences of maps with different scales.

- Draw the same three features (e.g., a house, a bridge and a school) as they would appear on three different maps with different scales.

- Predict which features would appear on large-scale maps compared to those that would appear on small-scale maps.

- *Assess the problems Google and other companies encounter when creating maps.*

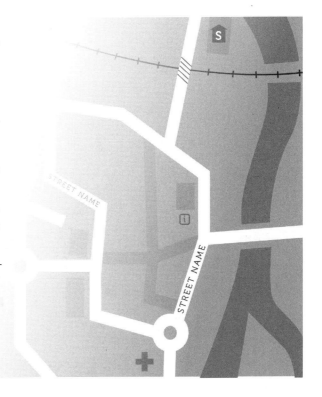

4.4.13 • Personal, Social and Health Education

Six- to nine-year-olds

Learning Intention

To <u>value and respect</u> the similarities and differences in our community

Success Criteria

To reach our learning goal, we will be able to:

- <u>Recognize</u> that there are similarities and differences between all of us.

- <u>Know</u> that different things contribute to our identity, including our membership in different groups.

- <u>Listen</u> respectfully to the viewpoints of others and speak with care and kindness.

- <u>Give examples</u> of basic needs and rights of all humans.

- <u>Demonstrate</u> respect for differences and communicate this with others.

- <u>Understand</u> that some people are threatened by difference.

4.4.14 • Christmas

Seven- to nine-year-olds

Learning Intention

To <u>understand the significance</u> to Christians of the key features of the nativity story

Success Criteria

To reach our learning goal, we will be able to:

- <u>Identify and explain</u> the symbolism conveyed by the characters in the story (e.g., ordinariness of shepherds representing common man, three wise men representing the three known continents at the time of Asia, Africa and Europe).

- <u>Empathize</u> with the feelings and responses of the characters in the nativity story.

- <u>Describe</u> *the meaning of the nativity story, saying how important the symbolism is.*

4.4.15 • Easter

Eight- to ten-year-olds

Learning Intention

To <u>make sense of</u> the events of Palm Sunday; to <u>interpret</u> the atmosphere and feelings of the crowd on Palm Sunday; to <u>recognize</u> how emotions are influenced by faith

Success Criteria

To reach our learning goal, we will be able to:

- <u>Connect</u> the Palm Sunday traditions with the story of how Jesus was welcomed as the Messiah (e.g., he's not the messiah; he's a very naughty boy).

- <u>Recount</u> the story of Palm Sunday.

- <u>Summarize</u> the feelings and expectations of the crowd.

- <u>Explore</u> the feelings of Jesus as he faced death.

- *Find examples of similar traditions in other religions.*

4.4.16 • Eid

Eight- to ten-year-olds

Learning Intention

To <u>understand why</u> Muslims celebrate Eid

Success Criteria

To reach our learning goal, we will be able to:

- <u>Demonstrate</u> an understanding of the key points raised in the Eid video.

- <u>Generate questions</u> about the video.

- <u>Give reasons why</u> Muslims celebrate Eid.

- <u>Explain</u> the key events and activities during Eid.

- *Compare what a Christian does during a celebration day with what a Muslim does during a celebration day by making timelines.*

4.4.17 • Diwali

Eight- to ten-year-olds

Learning Intention

To <u>find out about</u> the key events of Diwali and the story of Rama and Sita

Success Criteria

To reach our learning goal, we will be able to:

- <u>Identify</u> key events associated with the story.
- <u>Decode</u> the moral of the story.
- <u>Communicate</u> our responses to the behavior of the characters in the story.
- <u>Recount</u> the story using text and pictures.
- *<u>Account for</u> the feelings and motivations of the characters.*

4.4.18 • Religious Studies: Hinduism

Eight- to ten-year-olds

Learning Intention

To <u>understand the meaning</u> of the "aum" symbol and its <u>significance</u> for Hindus; to <u>know about</u> some aspects of Hindus' belief in God

Success Criteria

To reach our learning goal, we will be able to:

- <u>Explain</u> the beliefs that underlie the Hindu concept of God.
- <u>Reflect</u> on different ways of expressing beliefs about God.
- <u>Use</u> religious words accurately when explaining the meaning of worship.
- <u>Identify</u> the names of some of the Hindu Gods and Goddesses.
- *<u>Find links</u> between the Hindu Gods and the Viking and Roman Gods that we studied last year.*

4.5 • EXAMPLE LI AND SC TO USE WITH ELEVEN- TO EIGHTEEN-YEAR-OLDS

Here are some examples of LI and SC we have used recently with secondary school students.

Unlike with the primary school examples, we have not identified any age ranges. This is partly because stage is more influential than age but also because the secondary school teachers we know teach right across the age range and will therefore know which of their students the examples will work best with.

In this set of examples, the underlined words do not refer to the language of learning as they did in Section 4.4. Instead they show the attitudes that could be part of ASK model lessons (see Section 5.4 to read about the ASK Model).

> The underlined words in this section show an emphasis on attitudes.

The *bullet points in italics* are suggestions for extension criteria (see Section 4.2.5).

4.5.1 • Math: Trigonometry

Learning Intention

To understand how to use sine, cosine and tangent

Success Criteria

To reach our learning goal, we will be able to:

- Locate the sine, cosine and tangent in a right angled triangle.
- Explain what *sohcahtoa* stands for.
- Strive for accuracy when solving problems using trigonometric ratios.
- *Justify why the sin, cos and tan functions are important.*

4.5.2 • Literacy: Metaphors and Similes

Learning Intention

To develop an awareness of the use and construction of metaphors and similes

Success Criteria

To reach our learning goal, we will be able to:

- Identify what a simile is and what it does.
- Identify what a metaphor is and what it does.
- Compare and contrast similes and metaphors and their uses and effects.
- Recognize metaphors in a piece of text (Shakespeare's sonnet 73).
- Be willing to discuss Shakespeare's use of the metaphors in the sonnet.
- *Write three of our own metaphors based on three examples from the Shakespearean sonnet and their meanings.*

4.5.3 • Science: Forces

Learning Intentions

To <u>show an interest</u> in understanding what "upthrust" is and how it affects objects immersed in water

Success Criteria

To reach our learning goal, we will be able to:

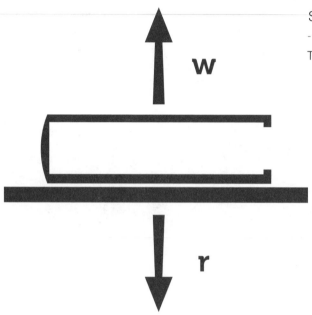

- Explain the link between "upthrust" and an object's weight.

- Justify why all objects weigh less in water than they do in air.

- Predict how much an object weighs when floating in water.

- Show the causal link between an object's density and whether or not it floats.

- Formulate the relationship between mass, density and volume.

- *Contrast the differences between the effect on weight when in water compared to when "walking" on the moon.*

4.5.4 • Religious Studies: Places of Worship

Learning Intention

To <u>show respect for others</u> by explaining the significance of key features of a place of worship in Judaism, Christianity and Islam

Success Criteria

To reach our learning goal, we will be able to:

- Analyze pictures and diagrams of places of worship across the world.

- Locate the parts of a place of worship and explain their significance.

- Ask appropriate questions about the place of worship and select relevant information to answer them.

- Construct a Venn diagram to show the similarities and differences of the key features between the different religions mentioned.

- *Imagine and plan a new place of worship with labels and explanations for each design feature.*

4.5.5 • History: Slavery

Learning Intentions

To learn about the range of indigenous groups across the continent of Africa and identify how slavery affected them in different ways

Success Criteria

To reach our learning goal, we will be able to:

- Use a range of maps to locate some of the different regional groupings across the African continent.

- Relate the main differences in features of regional groups (e.g., North African and sub-Saharan) to the physical environment.

- Illustrate with reference to European shipping routes and trade winds which regional groups were most at risk from slave traders.

- <u>Show an openness to understanding</u> how the negative effects of slavery can still be felt today.

- *Construct an overview of fifteenth-century African society.*

4.5.6 • Physical Education: Strategy

Learning Intentions

To apply principles of performance to plan tactics and strategies; to adapt strategies taking account of your own strengths and weaknesses and changing conditions and situations

Success Criteria

To reach our learning goal, we will be able to:

- Select appropriate approaches for the event.

- Distribute effort effectively within a competition.

- Choose when to use power and when to use greater control.

- Vary pace while keeping our form.

- <u>Take responsible risks</u> in varying effort, speed and power to identify the effect on performance.

- Decide upon starting positions for different tasks and events.

- *Think about how to split distance or time in terms of effort, speed and individual share.*

- *Discriminate between technical control and power in throwing events.*

4.5.7 • ICT: Filmmaking

Learning Intention

To produce creative and effective short online films

Success Criteria

To reach our learning goal, we will be able to:

- Highlight in the script the words and phrases that should be emphasized in the film.

- Plan the film schedule to ensure the footage will bring the script to life.

- Record clearly spoken audio tracks (loud, clear, appropriate pace and expression).

- <u>Persevere</u> with edit after edit until the film is just right.

- Edit the film to ensure it flows in a way that voices and visuals are highlighted.

- Add appropriate transitions, text, music and sound effects.

- <u>Learn from previous mistakes</u> by ensuring that extra effects add to overall effectiveness rather than distract or detract from the main message.

- Export the film in a format that can be readily played on mobile devices.

4.5.8 • Art: Impact on the Audience

Learning Intention

To <u>consider our impact on others</u> by examining the way in which our work might be received

Success Criteria

To reach our learning goal, we will be able to:

- Discuss our use of photographic and digital imaging techniques and how these provide different ways to represent life.

- Analyze how we have used visual and tactile qualities in our work.

- <u>Contribute constructively</u> to pair or group activities.

- Evaluate our own work and the ways in which we have sought to connect with our audience.

- Ask questions about others' work using appropriate terminology.

- Explain how our images symbolize personal interests.

- *Predict what overall impact our work has on others.*

- *Be aware of how powerfully our work projects the sense of self to others.*

4.5.9 • Music: Ternary Form

Learning Intention

Exercise curiosity by examining ternary form as a musical structure

Success Criteria

To reach our learning goal, we will be able to:

- Sing and play music in ternary form, recognizing when the first section is repeated by emphasizing the beginning of the repeat.

- Compose music using ternary form, making contrasted sections with some musical links.

- Listen to and analyze examples recorded using ternary form.

- *Identify any other music that uses two main ideas (e.g., verse and chorus).*

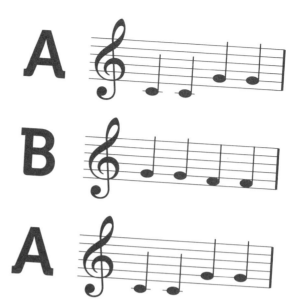

4.5.10 • Geography: Brazil

Learning Intention

Identify regional differences within the country of Brazil and their causes and consequences

Success Criteria

To reach our learning goal, we will be able to:

- Name and locate the five regions of Brazil, noting their key human and physical features (e.g., gas, oil, population density).

- Summarize key points in note form on an outline map showing regions, or produce a verbal report on this for TV or radio.

- Compare and contrast in depth two regions in Brazil.

- Describe, explain and compare in discussion and in continuous writing the causes and effects of changes in population in two of the selected regions.

- *Rank the five regions according to criteria you select and then be a critical friend when listening to the choices made by other groups.*

4.5.11 • Personal, Social and Health Education: Conflict and Resolution

Learning Intention

To define conflict and learn about different types of conflict

Success Criteria

To reach our learning goal, we will be able to:

- Work together to discuss and question our interpretation of conflict in the pictures.

- Consider other situations of conflict we know about, including local, regional, national and international situations.

- Define conflict.

- Justify and criticize the causes of conflict.

- <u>Question your own response</u> to conflict recently and think how you could make changes in the future.

- Understand how conflict begins and how it can affect different communities.

- *Decide whether conflict is always a bad thing or not.*

4.6 • LEARNING GOALS FOR WORKING TOGETHER

> Learning Intentions and Success Criteria can also focus on how students are learning rather than (or as well as) on what they are learning.

> A Diamond 9 can be used to help students select a few Success Criteria from a larger set.

The examples given in Sections 4.4 and 4.5 show a range of LI and SC covering the development of skills and knowledge. The secondary set in Section 4.5 also draws attention to the attitudes that might be used as learning goals. More about this can be seen in Section 5.4, which discusses the ASK model.

Another category that hasn't been explored yet relates to process-driven goals about how groups might collaborate together. This is explored in depth in Chapter 5 of *Challenging Learning Through Dialogue* (Nottingham et al., 2017). Linked to the ideas about groupings for dialogue explored in that book, Figure 9 shows the sort of success criteria you could use to help your students work effectively together.

We have drawn Figure 9 as a Criteria Diamond. It does not need to be drawn this way, but it can help your students in the following ways:

- Nine criteria are too many for students to concentrate on in just one session, so they can choose fewer (e.g., three) to focus on at any one time.

- The diamond shape gives the sense of hierarchy, with the top one being the most important, the next two being of equal second importance, the next three being of equal third importance and so on. You can choose to focus your students' attention on the hierarchy or not—whatever suits your purpose.

- Your students could pick one criterion from the top three, one from the middle three and one from the bottom three. Or Group A could take the top three, Group B could take the middle three and Group C could take the bottom three.

- Over a number of sessions, each group could ensure that they focus on all nine criteria (just as an athlete might focus on one or two parts of performance in each training session to improve the whole over time).

Please note that the way in which we have placed the criteria in Figure 9 is merely an example. Feel free to rearrange them to suit your purpose. Or even better, ask your students to rank the behaviors according to how important they think each one is to effective collaboration.

▶ Figure 9: Criteria for Collaborating Effectively

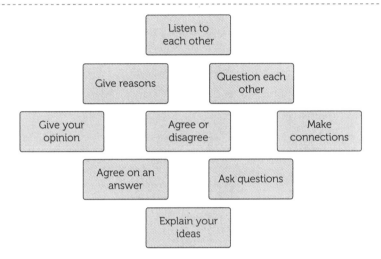

4.7 • REVIEW

This chapter has covered the following main points:

1. Feedback should always refer to the learning goals.

2. Without clear Learning Intentions (LI) and Success Criteria (SC), it is very difficult to generate high-quality, productive feedback.

3. Learning Intentions describe what students should know, understand or be able to do by the end of the lesson or series of lessons.

4. Success Criteria summarize the key steps or ingredients students need to accomplish the Learning Intention. They comprise the main things to do, include or focus on.

5. LI and SC do not hamper creativity—at least they shouldn't if used correctly.

6. LI and SC should always be understood by students, matched to individual's needs, connected to big, worthwhile ideas and meaningful to students' lives.

7. LI and SC don't just have to relate to short-term or time-specific goals, they can also relate to long-term aims such as helping students be more curious, persistent, self-regulating and willing to learn.

8. LI and SC can help teachers design effective learning activities for their students.

9. LI and SC can give students an understanding of what they are aiming to achieve (LI) and what they can do to reach their goal (SC).

10. LI and SC offer students language with which to articulate their learning.

11. SMART LI and SC are Specific, Measurable, Achievable or Aspirational, Relevant and Timely.

12. Using LI and SC as part of a preview for learning can be an effective way to help students make more progress.

4.8 • NEXT STEPS

Here are some suggestions to help you with your reflections on feedback:

1. What was your reaction to the house-drawing exercise? How much better could your feedback have been if you'd known the LI and SC beforehand?

2. Read through the example LI and SC shown in Sections 4.4 and 4.5, and choose one or two to try with your students.

3. Reflect on how well they worked with your students and what you could do to improve them for next time.

4. Have a go at co-creating some LI and SC with your students (see Section 4.2.2).

5. Try a preview activity with your students, and note the effects it has on the progress they make (see Section 4.2.6)

6. Design some LI and SC for your students, then check to see how SMART they are (see Section 4.3.2B)

7. Develop a set of long-term goals with your students, and then pay attention to the opportunities for giving them feedback related to those goals.

> "What students should learn first is not the subjects ordinarily taught, however important they may be; they should be given lessons of will, of attention, of discipline; before exercises in grammar, they need to be exercised in mental orthopaedics; in a word they must learn how to learn."
>
> (Binet, 1909)

TAXONOMIES TO SUPPORT GOAL SETTING

Taxonomies are general classifications representing the intended outcomes of the educational process. In the field of education, they are most often used to help learners identify the steps needed to develop a particular competence, and can be very useful when designing broad and balanced Learning Intentions (LI) and Success Criteria (SC).

Taxonomies can be very useful for helping you develop a wide range of Learning Intentions and Success Criteria. They can ensure that your students know *how* to learn as well as *what* to learn.

5.0 • LEARNING *HOW* TO LEARN

Learning how to learn is a process in which we all engage throughout our lives, although we often don't realize we are doing it. Most of the time we concentrate on *what* we are learning rather than *how* we are learning it. However, if we focus deliberately on ways *of* learning and teach students the skills and principles *for* learning, then we can increase the rate and depth at which they learn *how* to learn.

In a sense, learning how to learn is a process of discovery about learning. It involves a set of principles and skills that, if understood and applied, can help your students learn more effectively.

> Taxonomies can help students learn how to learn as well as *what* to learn. They can also be used to generate the right feedback at the right time for the right student.

> Students who learn how to learn are more effective learners and achieve better results.

At its heart is the belief that learning is learnable.

Learning-to-learn strategies—also known as metacognition and self-regulation approaches—have very high impact on learning. Indeed, a number of systematic reviews and meta-analyses have consistently found high levels of impact for strategies related to metacognition and self-regulation. And although most of these studies have looked at impact on language or mathematics, there is evidence from other subject areas, such as science, that suggests the approach is widely applicable.

Analysis of results from the PISA showed that the difference in reading performance between those students who generally know how to learn and those who don't was 107 points—the equivalent of more than two years of schooling (Organisation for Economic Co-operation and Development, 2013).

One of the reasons why some students fail to learn how to learn quite as well as others has to do with them taking more responsibility for their own learning. Thankfully, though, there are many things we can do to help—starting with leading less and scaffolding more.

Some of us in the teaching profession are guilty of supporting students too much. This stops our students from monitoring and managing their own learning. That is where scaffolding provides a useful metaphor: providing support when first introducing students to a concept, then stepping back bit by bit so that the students learn to manage their learning independently.

Taxonomies for learning can also help. Though some people are suspicious of taxonomies because of their supposed negative influence on creativity, a well-designed and properly used taxonomy can really help your students identify the strategies needed for learning how to learn. Taxonomies can show a beginner how to start filling a page or taking an action. They can help a proficient performer take the necessary steps to master a skill. And they can help experts reflect on why they are so good at what they do and how they can help others. They can also help you, the teacher, design Learning Intentions and Success Criteria that will teach your students *how* to learn as well as *what* to learn.

5.1 • USING TAXONOMIES WISELY

> For the right student, at the right time, taxonomies can be very helpful. But use them too often and students can become overreliant on them.

Some people are suspicious of taxonomies. They claim taxonomies hamper creativity. They worry taxonomies suppress individual expression. They liken taxonomies to "painting by numbers." This, however, misses the point and the purpose of taxonomies.

A well-designed and properly used taxonomy can help your students take their next steps to improved competence. They will rarely show everything your students will need to know and to do. But at the right time, for the right purpose, taxonomies can be very effective as an aid to teaching your students *how* to learn. Figure 10 and the corresponding discussion should help to identify when to use taxonomies.

► Figure 10: Using Taxonomies Correctly

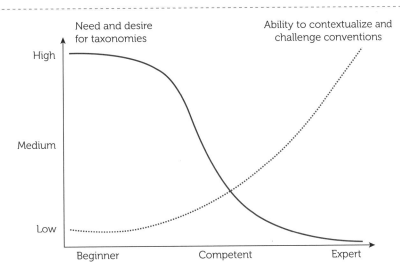

Looking at Figure 10, you can see that the x-axis shows the progression in capability from beginner to expert. The y-axis shows a simple scale from high to low.

Now look at the darker line. This shows the relative need and desire for taxonomies. When someone is a beginner, they need a taxonomy to know what to do. As they develop in confidence and competence, the need for this taxonomy wears off and is replaced by the ability to create and contextualize (shown by the lighter line).

> Beginners learn most from taxonomies. Experts have little need for them.

Stages of Development Affecting the Need for and Usefulness of Taxonomies

Absolute Beginner

Needs a Taxonomy

- needs generalized rules and structures
- without the "recipe," doesn't know what to do
- if something goes wrong, blames the taxonomy or the teacher
- takes very little responsibility

Beginner

Hungering for Certainty

- is starting to know the taxonomy
- wishes outcomes were more predictable
- wants the "expert" to fix things when something goes wrong
- still feels limited responsibility

Competent

- -

Planned and Analytical

- can assess the relative importance and urgency of each part of the taxonomy

- is able to adjust or change the taxonomy to suit his or her purpose

- can remember the original taxonomy and how it helped

- feels responsible for outcomes

Proficient

- -

Able to Adjust According to Context

- is seldom surprised, having learned what to expect

- has no need or desire for the original taxonomy

- displays rapid, fluid and intuitive behavior that would be hard to capture in a taxonomy

- sometimes forgets that others need a taxonomy to get started

Expert

- -

Does the Right Thing at the Right Time

- is highly intuitive, based on a huge store of wisdom

- has a great capacity for handling the unexpected

- suffers if generalized rules are imposed

- engages in highly nuanced behavior that cannot be captured in a taxonomy

So, as you can see, taxonomies have a limited "shelf life." However, we should not dismiss their potential because of this. Instead, we ought to recognize them for what they are: an excellent way to help our students grow in competence and understanding.

(James) My wife and eldest daughter love to watch *The Great British Bake Off* on TV. Personally, I don't understand what is so fascinating about watching people baking cakes. Whenever I end up watching it, it just makes me hungry!

Anyway, one of the frequent sources of amusement for both my wife and daughter is to suppose just how pathetic I would be as a contestant on that program. And they're right—I really would have no clue where to start.

That is unless Mary (apparently half of Britain are on first-name terms with the matriarch of the program, Mary Berry) gave me the ingredients and a foolproof recipe! Then I would have a good chance at making something reasonably edible.

> Taxonomies are like recipes: they show novices how to achieve a goal but are of little use to experts.

And that's the point of taxonomies: they are just like the recipe for baking a cake. They should show a complete novice like me the steps to take in order to succeed with a task. And just like a recipe, they become less and less necessary as the user grows in competence.

5. Taxonomies to Support Goal Setting

Imagine how patronizing it would be to suggest that Mary Berry would succeed only if she follows the recipe: "Mary—now here's the flour, egg and water. What I want you to do is crack the egg over the side of the bowl and pour it gently into the flour. . . ." I'd be amazed if the dear lady didn't fling the flour in my face!

Keeping with this theme and looking again at the stages of development we just discussed, as an absolute beginner, I very definitely need the recipe. And if it all goes wrong, then I am likely to blame outside influences such as someone else opening the oven door or the scales needing replacing.

My eldest daughter, on the other hand, is probably more at stage 2 of development with baking—a beginner in search of certainty. She's starting to know various recipes and can have a good go at baking a number of different cakes. However, when things go wrong she's not sure why they have and so turns to her mother for help.

If my daughter keeps going with baking, then she should quite quickly pass on to the competent stage. This will be when she can begin to tailor the recipe to suit her taste buds (more chocolate, less fruit and nuts, I suspect). She will also be able to plan better for baking and need her mother's supervision less and less.

My wife is probably at the proficient stage. She makes some lovely cakes and loves to experiment by altering recipes, measuring things out intuitively rather than relying on scales, and seldom being surprised at different outcomes.

Mary, of course, is an expert. She always knows exactly why a contestant's cake hasn't turned out quite as perfect as her demo did. She has a wonderful way of handling the unexpected. And hell's bells, she's made a fortune from writing a whole array of recipes. She also happens to be the type of grandma that every child would wish for—but that's another story.

Just a thought to finish: Where are you on the proficiency scale? Not so much with baking (unless you want to think about that). But what about with teaching? Or with handling disruptive students? Or with generating high-quality feedback?

And what could you do next to move on to the next level of proficiency with each of these?

5.2 • BLOOM'S TAXONOMY (AND BEYOND)

Perhaps the best-known taxonomy in education is Bloom's taxonomy. Having said that, when people refer to "Bloom's taxonomy," they are generally talking about his taxonomy of thinking skills. Actually, Benjamin Bloom and his colleagues proposed three domains: cognitive, affective and psychomotor. These are shown in Figure 11.

> Bloom's taxonomy originally focused on three domains: cognitive, affective and psychomotor.

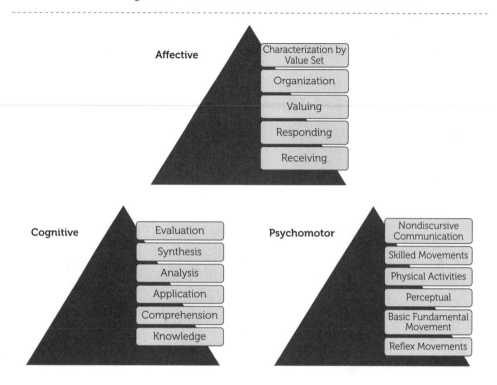

By focusing on Attitudes, Skills and Knowledge, the ASK model is the modern equivalent of Bloom's taxonomy of Cognitive, Affective and Psychomotor domains.

Matthew Lipman, creator of Philosophy for Children, argued that the Cognitive domain of Bloom's taxonomy should also include Reasoning.

Perhaps one of the reasons that this broad range of educational objectives is less well known than the thinking skills dimension is that Bloom and his colleagues produced a more elaborate compilation for the cognitive domain than they did for the other two. Indeed, they never really developed a full analysis of the psychomotor domain, saying that they had had very little experience of teaching manual skills!

And yet, for Learning Intentions and Success Criteria—and indeed education in general—to be holistic, perhaps we ought to pay close attention to all three domains.

It is for this very reason that we recommend the use of the ASK model (see Section 5.4). By renaming Bloom's domains from Affective to Attitudes, Psychomotor to Skills, and Cognitive to Knowledge, we are able to make reference to the ASK model. Of course, the Cognitive domain pays attention to much more than just Knowledge, but at least ASK is more user-friendly than Bloom's original set of domains!

At the risk of turning this chapter into a criticism of Bloom's work (and that is definitely not our intention), the Cognitive domain of Bloom's work virtually ignores reasoning (and therefore reasonableness), although many people would say reasoning is a part of all the other categories of thinking, particularly the comprehension, analysis and evaluation dimensions. But as Matthew Lipman, the creator of Philosophy for Children and one of the twentieth century's most respected educational theorists, put it, "Bloom's Taxonomy of Educational Objectives virtually ignores reasoning skills. In light of this, one must wonder how it achieved the canonical position it has held for the past quarter-century" (Lipman & Sharp, 1986).

Another problem (sometimes) is that Bloom and his colleagues presented the Cognitive domain as a hierarchy with knowledge at the bottom and evaluation at the top. This can have its benefits, some of which are explored in *Challenging Learning Through Questioning* (Nottingham & Renton, in press). But for the purposes of generating Learning Intentions and Success Criteria, and identifying the language to use when giving feedback, we find it more useful to dispense with the hierarchy.

So for the purposes of this book, if we flatten the hierarchy and then add in the seventh dimension of reasoning, then the Nottingham version of Bloom's taxonomy would look something like Figure 12.

▶ **Figure 12: The Nottingham Version of Bloom's Taxonomy**

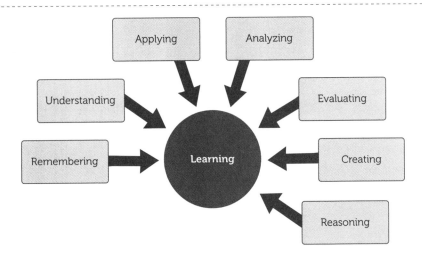

These dimensions are each broken down over the next few pages. For the purpose of generating Learning Intentions and Success Criteria, they are written in alphabetical order rather than hierarchically as with Bloom's original work.

Analyzing

Terms to use in Learning Intentions and Success Criteria when you want your students to show they are able to analyze ideas and find evidence to support generalizations:

- analyze
- breakdown
- categorize
- classify
- compare
- contrast
- deconstruct
- draw
- examine
- experiment
- predict
- represent
- resolve
- sequence
- subdivide
- rank

Many of the verbs shown could appear in more than one category. So to avoid repetition, each verb has been placed where it fits best.

Applying

Terms to use in Learning Intentions and Success Criteria when you want your students to apply their knowledge and understanding to other situations:

- apply
- change
- construct
- demonstrate
- dramatize
- employ
- extend
- illustrate
- interpret
- manipulate
- operate
- organize
- practice
- produce
- use
- write

Creating

Terms to use in Learning Intentions and Success Criteria when you want your students to pull together component ideas into a new whole:

- arrange
- assemble
- combine
- compose
- create
- design
- devise
- elaborate
- formulate
- generate
- modify
- prepare
- rearrange
- reconstruct
- relate
- reorganize

Evaluating

Terms to use in Learning Intentions and Success Criteria when you want your students to show that they can make or test judgments against agreed-upon criteria:

- assess
- calculate
- conclude
- criticize
- critique
- defend
- discriminate
- estimate
- evaluate
- exemplify
- judge
- justify
- rate
- summarize
- support
- value

Reasoning

Terms to use in Learning Intentions and Success Criteria when you want your students to show that they are able to rationalize and interpret:

- choose
- connect
- decide
- deduce
- determine
- generalize
- give reasons
- hypothesize
- prove
- question
- rationalize
- show cause
- solve
- suppose
- test
- verify

Remembering

Terms to use in Learning Intentions and Success Criteria when you want your students to remember previous learned information:

- identify
- label
- list
- match
- memorize
- name
- order
- outline
- recall
- recognize
- recollect
- remember
- repeat
- reproduce
- select
- state

Understanding

Terms to use in Learning Intentions and Success Criteria when you want your students to demonstrate an understanding of the facts:

- accept
- appreciate
- comprehend
- describe
- discuss
- distinguish
- explain
- give examples
- infer
- locate
- paraphrase
- rewrite
- review
- show
- show how
- translate

5.3 • THE EDUCERE TAXONOMY OF THINKING SKILLS

To some people, teaching students how to learn begins with developing thinking dispositions such as curiosity, strategy and open-mindedness. Other people begin by focusing on skills such as locating relevant information, comparing, synthesizing and understanding. Bloom emphasizes higher-order thinking, whereas Matthew Lipman promotes critical, creative and caring thinking.

We have synthesized all of these approaches to create the EDUCERE Taxonomy of Thinking Skills. *Educere* is the Latin word from which the English word *education* comes, so we hope that the acronym is easy to remember.

Engage

Desire

Understand

Create

Enquire

Reason

Evaluate

You can use this taxonomy when designing Learning Intentions and Success Criteria. You could also share the taxonomy with your students so that they know what attitudes, skills and knowledge they will need to develop if they are to learn how to learn.

> The EDUCERE taxonomy brings together a comprehensive list of thinking skills to help students learn how to learn. Each category can also be used as a guide to generate high-quality feedback.

Engage

Paying attention and thinking collaboratively with:

- verbal acts such as saying, asserting, proposing, hinting, inferring, alleging and contending

- mental acts such as focusing, committing energy and enthusiasm, and maintaining concentration

- physical acts involving positive and interested body language

Desire

Having the inclination and desire to:

- wonder and enquire

- reflect upon and evaluate ideas and performances

- take responsibility as well as calculated risks

- work collaboratively as well as independently

- imagine new possibilities and be open-minded

- be resilient and tenacious

- manage emotions and impulses

- be thoughtful

Understand

Understanding information by:

- locating relevant data
- seeking clarity and precision
- comparing and contrasting
- sorting and classifying
- sequencing
- making connections
- representing information
- seeking deeper understandings
- identifying misconceptions

Create

Creating new ideas by:

- looking for alternatives and possibilities
- generating hypotheses
- innovating
- assembling and formulating
- suspending logic temporarily
- searching for value
- thinking flexibly
- asking "What if?"

Enquire

Enquiring into the current subject matter by:

- asking relevant questions
- defining problems
- predicting outcomes
- testing conclusions
- seeking details to give depth
- interpreting meaning

Reason

Developing reasoning by:

- giving reasons
- using precise language
- inferring and deducing
- applying logic

- testing assumptions
- presenting balanced arguments

Evaluate

Judging the value of something by:

- developing criteria
- checking accuracy
- identifying improvements
- testing relevance and significance
- benchmarking
- comparing with alternatives

5.4 • THE ASK MODEL

The ASK model first appeared in *Challenging Learning* (Nottingham, 2010a). It was then published in *Encouraging Learning* (Nottingham, 2013) and then later in more depth in the second edition of *Challenging Learning* (Nottingham, 2016). It is also shown as a model for generating high-quality questions and challenge in another book in this new series: *Challenging Learning Through Questioning* (Nottingham & Renton, in press).

The model is now a very popular tool for helping teachers design a broad range of Learning Intentions and Success Criteria. It is also very useful for identifying a range of pedagogical questions and for determining whether lessons are holistic (as opposed to focusing exclusively on content).

The ASK model is a development of Bloom's Taxonomy of Educational Objectives (see Section 5.2). It brings together a focus on **A**ttitudes, **S**kills and **K**nowledge. For someone to learn how to learn (see Section 5.0), they will need to have positive attitudes toward learning, be skilful in a number of aspects of learning, and have good general knowledge and conceptual understanding so that they are able to find and assess information. Therefore, to grow into an expert learner, your students will need to develop expertise in all three domains:

> **Attitudes:** positive attitudes toward learning, including curiosity and persistence

> **Skills:** abilities to carry out those processes necessary for gaining understanding, taking part in dialogue and achieving excellent performance in any given field

> **Knowledge:** familiarity with information, concepts, theories and practices in a given field

> The ASK model brings together Attitudes, Skills and Knowledge. It can be used to plan lessons, design broad and balanced Learning Intentions and Success Criteria and generate high-quality feedback.

5.4.1 • Attitudes

Think of the difference between teaching thirty students who value learning and fifteen students who don't. Or compare the likely progress of a student who is easily discouraged with one who persists and overcomes challenges. It seems attitudes play a major role in the outcomes of education.

Many believe that a combination of genetic dispositions and upbringing will determine the extent to which students value learning. They argue that we can work with or against only what is already given. And yet, the evidence is clear: it is possible to develop excellent attitudes toward learning by modeling, articulating and teaching the attitudes you want your students to learn.

That is easier said than done, of course, since finding agreement about which attitudes are the "right" ones to promote is a challenge in itself. Help is on hand, though, as there are many sources of inspiration, including Art Costa's (2000) *Habits of Mind* and Guy Claxton's (2002) *Building Learning Power*.

A very effective approach is to draw out some ideas from your students. To do this, ask your students to consider the following:

- Think of a goal or target that you have achieved, for example, learning to ride your bike, reciting your times tables, playing a musical instrument, writing a poem, making friends at a new school.

- What attitudes helped you to achieve this?

Record the answers that your students come up with, and turn these into statements of intent (see below).

> Attitudes are not fixed. They can be encouraged, taught and developed. As such, they should form part of students' Learning Intentions and Success Criteria.

Sample Answers From Eleven-Year-Olds

- always trying hard
- being open to advice
- thinking carefully
- being willing to try new things
- having a never-say-die attitude
- learning from mistakes
- staying focused
- being open-minded

> Students often know the attitudes that are needed for success in learning. So rather than be given a set of attitudes to work on, students can be engaged in creating their own list.

Corresponding Statements of Intent

- We always try hard.
- We are open to advice, offering support to each other.
- We think carefully about our studies.
- We are willing to try new things.
- We are tenacious (have a never-say-die attitude).
- We treat mistakes as opportunities to learn.
- We concentrate and remain focused during our learning.
- We are open to new ideas and different opinions.

Of course, it is not enough simply to decide the attitudes you wish to develop and then display them in the classroom. If that were all it took, then every school with pretty dispositions posters (e.g., TEAM: Together Everyone Achieves More) would have perfect students with perfect attitudes!

So to have a better chance of embedding the attitudes you want, we recommend that you try the following:

1. Identify the attitudes that you wish to focus on, using the approach shown.

2. Display these attitudes on the wall and talk with your students about their meanings. This would include developing from straightforward definitions to elaborations, for example:

   • creating a poster to illustrate each of the attitudes

   • identifying key role models for each attitude (e.g., Winston Churchill or JK Rowling for determination)

   • exploring each attitude through storytelling, poetry, art or philosophical inquiry

3. Model each of the attitudes explicitly so it is obvious to your students how and when they are using each one to accomplish their learning goals.

4. Use every opportunity that presents itself to remind your students of the learning attitudes. For example, when they are stuck on a piece of work, remind them that this is an opportunity to practice perseverance.

5. Teach each of the attitudes as part of your Learning Intentions, using the ASK model.

5.4.2 • Skills

Skills are the abilities to carry out those processes necessary for gaining understanding, taking part in dialogue and achieving excellent performance in any given field. Children (and adults) develop their abilities through social interaction and from the social, cultural and educational context of their lives.

Intellectual Skills

These include identifying, modeling and altering relationships or concepts; understanding relevance; drawing conclusions; comparing and contrasting; asking relevant questions; hypothesizing

Social Skills

These include building rapport; respecting others' viewpoints; acting appropriately in particular contexts; self-regulating; working individually and as a team; encouraging others

Communicative Skills

These include being able to understand and be understood; listening and responding appropriately to others; talking persuasively and respectfully; requesting things politely; paying full attention to a speaker; reading body language

Physical Skills

These include coordinating actions needed for such things as penmanship; manipulating objects to represent ideas; catching and throwing an object; dancing; drama; riding a bicycle; making art; playing a sport

Specialized Skills

These include the abilities we need for specific types of action such as driving a car; using a map and compass, a ruler or tape measure, a paint brush, sporting equipment, weighing scales, a computer mouse

> There are many categories of skills that help students move closer to their learning goals. These include intellectual, social, communication and physical skills. There are also less generalized skills (e.g., map reading, using a ruler and protractor correctly).

Note: we've included social skills because although many people will say that getting along with others has more to do with attitude than skill, we're not sure this is the case. It seems that both attitudes and skills affect behavior. For example, one of your students may have a very friendly disposition but not, as yet, the ability to make friends. And of course the reverse might also be true: one of your students may know perfectly well how to make friends but does not have the inclination to do so. Therefore, a lesson focusing on how to build rapport with another person or how to begin a conversation with another person will develop very important life skills that many of your students might not have learned yet.

5.4.3 • Knowledge

We are assuming that each country or state has its own curriculum that identifies the knowledge that students are required to learn. So for that reason, we have not broken Knowledge down into parts as we did with Attitudes and Skills.

5.4.4 • Designing LI and SC Using the ASK Model

The ASK model can be used to ensure a breadth and variety of Learning Intentions and Success Criteria. These in turn help to generate high-quality feedback.

Once you have identified the attitudes and skills you think your students should learn, then you can use the ASK model to plan some varied and balanced LI and SC.

We find it useful to draw the ASK model as a triangle and then place a cross on the part of the diagram that relates to relative balance between attitudes, skills and knowledge. For example, looking at Figure 13, Lesson 1 focuses primarily on an Attitude but also has SC to do with Skills; Lesson 2 is more about Skills but also about Knowledge; and Lesson 3 gives equal weight to Attitudes and Knowledge.

▶ **Figure 13: The ASK Model**

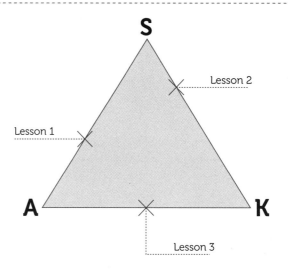

Lesson 1: Emphasis on Attitude, with acknowledgment of a Skill

> LI: To exercise our curiosity (Attitude: curiosity) about the Vikings
>
> SC: Generate at least nine relevant questions (Skill: asking relevant questions) about Vikings' lifestyles.

Lesson 2 (or part 2 of the same lesson): A Skill takes priority, with Knowledge as a secondary aim

> LI: To decide which of the questions about Vikings has the most relevance to our learning (Skill: prioritizing by value)
>
> SC: Identify at least one fact that each of the questions could lead us to discover (Knowledge: facts about the lifestyles of Vikings).

By varying the emphasis of Learning Intentions using the ASK model, learning (and therefore feedback) can be made more holistic.

Lesson 3: A balance between Knowledge and an Attitude

LI: To persist (Attitude: persistence) in trying to find answers to our questions

SC: Find credible answers (Knowledge: finding credible answers) to the top three questions we chose last time.

5.4.5 • Sample LI and SC Matched to the ASK Model

If you look at the sample Learning Intentions and Success Criteria in Section 4.5, you will see we have underlined the Attitudes used in each one. They are as follows:

4.5.1 Math: Trigonometry

- <u>Strive for accuracy</u> when solving problems using trigonometric ratios.

4.5.2 Literacy: Metaphors and Similes

- <u>Be willing</u> to discuss Shakespeare's use of the metaphors in the sonnet.

4.5.3 Science: Forces

- To <u>show an interest</u> in understanding what "upthrust" is and how it affects objects immersed in water

4.5.4 Religious Studies: Places of Worship

- To <u>show respect for others</u> by explaining the significance of key features of a place of worship in Judaism, Christianity and Islam

4.5.5 History: Slavery

- <u>Show an openness to understanding</u> how the negative effects of slavery can still be felt today.

4.5.6 Physical Education: Strategy

- <u>Take responsible risks</u> in varying effort, speed and power to identify the effect on performance.

4.5.7 ICT: Filmmaking

- <u>Persevere</u> with edit after edit until the film is just right.

- <u>Learn from previous mistakes</u> by ensuring that extra effects add to overall effectiveness rather than distract or detract from the main message.

4.5.8 Art: Impact on the Audience

- To <u>consider our impact on others</u> by examining the way in which our work might be received

- <u>Contribute constructively</u> to pair or group activities.

4.5.9 Music: Ternary Form

- <u>Exercise curiosity</u> by examining ternary form as a musical structure

4.5.10 Geography: Brazil

- Rank the five regions according to criteria you select and then <u>be a critical friend</u> when listening to the choices made by other groups.

4.5.11 Personal, Social and Health Education: Conflict and Resolution

- <u>Question your own response</u> to conflict recently and think how you could make changes in the future.

5.5 • FOOTNOTE TO TAXONOMIES: BEWARE!

(James) In 2010, I made a speech at an education conference in Kuala Lumpur. The other keynote speaker was Howard Gardner, the creator of Multiple Intelligences. He began his presentation by saying, "I wish teachers had never heard my ideas about Multiple Intelligences because teachers are obsessed with categorizing kids."

Soon after that conference, I noticed a young man at the back of a math class who was flailing his arms around frenetically. All the other students were paying full attention to the teacher. This went on for a big chunk of the lesson. Afterward I asked the teacher whether this was normal, to which she replied, rather proudly, "Damian is a kinaesthetic learner. He learns better when he moves."

What a load of rubbish! The boy doesn't have a medical condition; he's simply been told he's a kinaesthetic learner and gone along with it because it sounds fun. His teacher had asked her students to complete a learning styles questionnaire and then concluded that some were visual learners, others were auditory and the rest were kinaesthetic. She'd gone on to declare that visual learners had to see something written down to learn well, auditory learners had to hear something and the kinaesthetic lot—well, they had to bop and groove to learn!

Don't get me wrong: I agree we all have preferences. I seem to remember things better if I've seen them written down, but it's not impossible for me to learn through listening, despite what my wife would tell you.

Similar issues have arisen from the use—or rather, misuse—of taxonomies. I've heard comments in schools such as "That child is a higher-order thinker!" Presumably this is intended to highlight the ability of that student to evaluate, synthesize and analyze, which is what Bloom regarded as higher-order thinking skills. Again, what a load of rubbish! Surely, a "higher-order thinker" (if such a person exists) is someone who uses the right type of thinking at the right time for the right purpose. For example, what would be the benefit of evaluating (a so-called higher-order skill) if all we wanted to do is "remember" (supposedly a lower-order thinking skill) somebody's name? If you were lost, I assume you would not ask the next passer-by, "What does it mean to be lost? Can we synthesize a new understanding of the term *lost*?" Surely you're just going to ask, "Which way should I go?" Which, though a supposedly "lower-order" thinking skill, is presumably a much more useful question to ask in the circumstances!

So let's not get carried away with taxonomies. They are there to support us, not to lead us. And they are certainly not there to categorize or label us.

Instead, pick and choose a few to begin with—starting with the many wonderful examples in this book. Then change them, bend them and adapt them to suit your context. They will help your students make progress and know which learning steps to take next. They will help us teachers and pedagogues plan for progression. But please remember, taxonomies should be servants to learning, not masters of schooling!

5.6 • REVIEW

This chapter has covered the following main points:

1. Taxonomies can be very useful for developing a wide range of Learning Intentions and Success Criteria.

2. Taxonomies can ensure that students know *how* to learn as well as *what* to learn.

3. A well-designed and properly used taxonomy can help students take their next steps to improved competence.

4. Taxonomies are like recipes, and beginners need the recipe.

5. Competent performers can tailor the recipe to suit themselves.

6. Proficient and expert performers do not need the recipe. Indeed, they are likely to feel restricted by a recipe.

7. Bloom's Taxonomy of Educational Objectives proposed three domains of learning: Cognitive, Affective and Psychomotor.

8. Bloom's taxonomy can be very useful for designing a wide range of Learning Intentions and Success Criteria.

9. The EDUCERE Taxonomy of Thinking Skills brings together the best approaches of lots of taxonomies for learning. It covers student Engagement, Desire, Understanding, Creativity, Enquiry, Reasoning and Evaluative skills.

10. The ASK model is a modern-day equivalent of Bloom's original taxonomy. It can be used to design LI and SC that cover Attitudes, Skills and Knowledge.

11. Skills can be subdivided into Intellectual, Social, Communicative, Physical and Specialized.

12. When drawn as a triangle, the ASK model provides a very useful planning tool to assist with the creation of a wide range of LI and SC.

5.7 • NEXT STEPS

Here are some suggestions to help you with your reflections on feedback:

1. Use Figure 10 to identify where you are in the stages of development for giving feedback.

2. Identify two or three actions you could take to move on to the next stage of development.

3. Over the next few weeks, design some LI and SC that use at least one verb from each of the seven categories in the Nottingham version of Bloom's taxonomy.

4. Display the EDUCERE Taxonomy of Thinking Skills in your classroom and invite your students to refer to it when they are giving themselves and each other feedback.

5. Use the ASK model to review the LI and SC you have used recently with your students. Are there more crosses on one side of the triangle than on the other sides?

"The bottom line: In most countries and economies, differences in reading performance between advantaged and disadvantaged students can be partly explained by how well students have learned how to learn by the time they are 15 years old. Parents and teachers can help to close this performance gap by **ensuring that all students know how best to approach learning.**"

(Organisation for Economic Co-operation and Development, 2013)

FEEDBACK AND THE SOLO TAXONOMY

6

6.0 • THE SOLO TAXONOMY

SOLO stands for Structure of Observed Learning Outcomes. John Biggs and Kevin Collis (1982) first described it in *Evaluating the Quality of Learning: The SOLO Taxonomy*.

The SOLO taxonomy provides a very useful reference point when describing your students' progress from no knowledge through to deep understanding. In brief, the SOLO taxonomy describes the levels shown in Figure 14 (illustrations provided by the Challenging Learning team).

> The SOLO taxonomy is a very useful way to describe different stages in learning.

► Figure 14: **The SOLO Taxonomy**

SOLO Stage

Prestructural

This is when your students have NO IDEA to connect to the intended learning.

Unistructural

This is when your students have ONE IDEA that connects with the intended learning.

Multistructural

This is when your students have MANY IDEAS that connect with the intended learning.

Relational

This is when your students are able to CONNECT & RELATE their ideas together.

Extended Abstract

This is when your students are able to EVALUATE & APPLY their ideas to new and different contexts.

The SOLO taxonomy has many uses, including the following:

1. Designing learning experiences matched to your students' current level of understanding

2. Writing Learning Intentions that have progression built into them (e.g., LI: To identify five effects of border controls and then relate them to current changes in the Schengen agreement)

3. Constructing Success Criteria that build understanding, for example:

   • Label the main parts of the water cycle (single idea recall)

   • Describe the importance of each part of the water cycle (drawing together many ideas about function and significance)

   • Explain how the water cycle works and the interaction between each of the parts you have labeled (making links and relating parts to the whole)

4. Creating a focus for feedback so that it is easier to move your students to their next stage of learning

5. Giving you and your students language to talk about progress in learning

6. Helping to make the most of the Learning Challenge (see Section 6.1)

> The SOLO taxonomy can be used as a guide for generating feedback that is matched to each stage of learning.

6.1 • HOW THE SOLO TAXONOMY RELATES TO THE LEARNING CHALLENGE

If you are already familiar with Challenging Learning's work, then you will notice that the SOLO taxonomy has a lot in common with the Learning Challenge (Nottingham, 2016, 2017).

The Learning Challenge helps teachers structure lessons and students challenge themselves (see Figure 15). It has been used successfully with three- to eighteen-year-olds and is now a reference point in hundreds of classrooms around the world. It can also be used to generate high-quality feedback questions.

You can find out more about the model in *The Learning Challenge* (Nottingham, 2017).

> The SOLO taxonomy fits very well with the Learning Challenge. Together these models provide a language for thinking about learning.

▶ Figure 15: **The Learning Challenge**

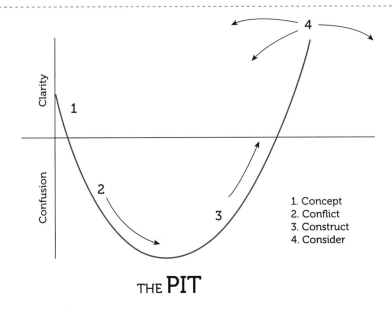

1. Concept
2. Conflict
3. Construct
4. Consider

THE **PIT**

The Learning Challenge has four stages:

Stage 1: Concept

The Learning Challenge begins with a concept. The concept can come from the media, conversation, observations or the curriculum. So as long as your students have at least some understanding of the concept, then the Learning Challenge can work.

Stage 2: Conflict

The key to the Learning Challenge is to get your students "into the pit" by creating cognitive conflict in their minds (Edwards, 2001; Nottingham, 2010a). This deliberate creation of a dilemma is what makes the Learning Challenge such a good model for challenge and inquiry.

Stage 3: Construct

After a while of being in the pit, some of your students will begin to construct meaning for themselves. They will do this by identifying relationships, explaining causes and

> Like the SOLO taxonomy, the Learning Challenge describes four main stages in the learning process.

integrating ideas into a new structure. As they do this, they will experience a sense of *eureka* in which they have a new sense of clarity. This in turn puts them in an ideal position to help those students who are still confused.

Stage 4: Consider

Once out of the pit, your students should be encouraged to reflect on the stages of thinking they've just been through—from a single, simplistic idea (Stage 1) to the identification of lots of sometimes conflicting ideas (Stage 2) right through to a new understanding of more complex and interrelated ideas (Stage 3). They should then look for ways to relate and apply their new understanding to different contexts.

The Learning Challenge is also included in Chapter 8 because of its use as a review tool.

We hope the brief overview above is enough to show you how much the Learning Challenge has in common with the SOLO taxonomy. To further develop your understanding, we have blended the two together over the next few pages.

Prestructural

No Idea Pit 0: Pre-Pit

▶ Figure 16: **The Learning Challenge and the Prestructural Phase of SOLO**

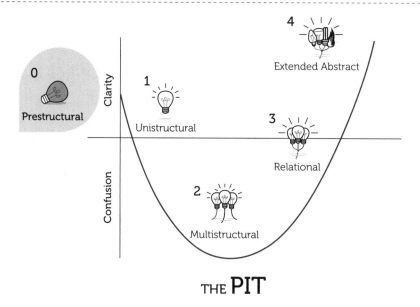

THE PIT

In the Prestructural phase of SOLO (before the Learning Challenge even begins), your students will do one or more of the following:

- say they have no idea
- attempt the task inappropriately

> The Prestructural phase of the SOLO taxonomy corresponds with a pre-Pit stage in which students have no knowledge about the topic or concept.

- identify irrelevant or incorrect information

- miss the point

- be unable (and perhaps unwilling) to make a start without a lot of support and encouragement

- say they need help

Unistructural

Basic Idea Pit 1: Start of the Pit

▶ Figure 17: **The Learning Challenge and the Unistructural Phase of SOLO**

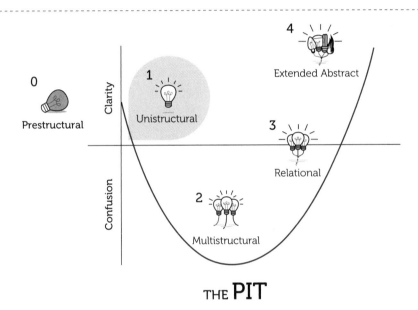

THE **PIT**

> The Unistructural phase of the SOLO taxonomy corresponds with Stage 1 of the Learning Challenge. At this point, students have a basic idea about the concept underpinning the current learning goals.

In the Unistructural phase of SOLO and the Concept stage of the Learning Challenge, your students will do one or more of the following:

- say they know something about the topic

- be able to identify, name, remember, match or list the basic items

- have a go at the task by following simple procedures

- attempt to achieve the first one or two Success Criteria

- identify relevant information

- begin to know the purpose of the task

Multistructural

Many Ideas Pit 2: In the Pit!

▶ **Figure 18: The Learning Challenge and the Multistructural Phase of SOLO**

The Multistructural phase of the SOLO taxonomy corresponds with Stage 2 of the Learning Challenge. At this point, students have many ideas about the concept(s) underpinning the current learning goals.

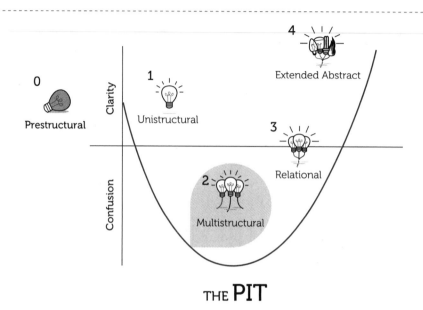

THE **PIT**

In the Multistructural phase of SOLO and the Conflict stage of the Learning Challenge, your students will do one or more of the following:

- find many more ideas

- be able to describe, compare, notice patterns and find exceptions

- engage animatedly in the task

- perhaps be frustrated by not having reached a conclusion yet

- develop their earlier ideas, adding complexity to their descriptions

- have a good sense of the relevance and purpose of the task

Relational

Connecting Ideas Pit 3: Coming Out of the Pit

▶ Figure 19: **The Learning Challenge and the Relational Phase of SOLO**

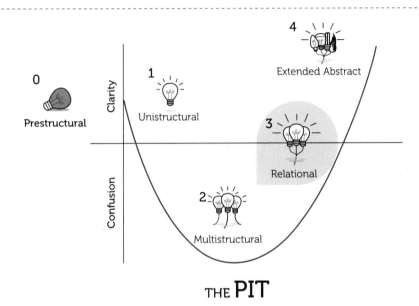

THE **PIT**

The Relational phase of the SOLO taxonomy corresponds with Stage 3 of the Learning Challenge. This is where students have their eureka moment in which they discover a sense of clarity about the meaning of their ideas and how they all relate to each other.

In the Relational phase of SOLO and the Construct stage of the Learning Challenge, your students will do one or more of the following:

- have a eureka moment
- connect their ideas together
- understand patterns and how the ideas relate to each other
- be able to explain the cause, effect and significance
- begin to organize, distinguish, relate and analyze
- explain to others what steps to take to make progress
- show a sense of achievement
- look for ways to share or apply their newfound understanding

Extended Abstract

Many Ideas Pit 4: Reviewing and Linking

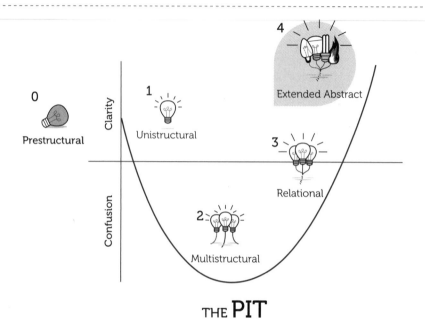

THE **PIT**

The Extended Abstract phase of the SOLO taxonomy corresponds with Stage 4 of the Learning Challenge. At this point, students have enough depth of understanding to be able to apply their ideas to new and different contexts.

In the Extended Abstract phase of SOLO and the Consider stage of the Learning Challenge, your students will do one or more of the following:

- review, relate and understand their learning journey
- apply their understanding to new and different contexts
- be able to generalize, hypothesize, prioritize, design, create, evaluate and perform
- explain how they developed their understanding and say what they could've done differently (e.g., how they could've made it more engaging, challenging, simple or inclusive)
- critique the process and strategies they used this time so as to identify how best to tackle other similar tasks
- create similar tasks or problems for others to try

6.2 • HOW THE SOLO TAXONOMY RELATES TO FEEDBACK

As we've shown throughout this book, there isn't one type or form of feedback that suits every occasion. However, the SOLO taxonomy can provide some guidance as to what is *likely to be* useful for your students at different stages of their learning.

▶ Figure 21: Feedback and the SOLO Taxonomy

The SOLO taxonomy helps to generate feedback that is matched closely to a student's stage of learning.

SOLO Stage	
Prestructural	**Prestructural** At this stage of the learning process, your students need your expert guidance. They are generally not ready for feedback yet. What will help them are clear Learning Intentions and Success Criteria. And probably lots of direct instruction!
Unistructural	**Unistructural** Generally, at this stage of the learning process, your students are best left to have a go at the task by themselves. They should have enough information to make a start but won't have done enough yet to warrant—or make good use of—feedback. Encouragement often helps, though!
Multistructural	**Multistructural** Your students may well appreciate some feedback at this stage, even if it is just to confirm they are on the right track. So this is often the perfect time to get them to engage in some self- or peer-review feedback. See Step 3 of the Seven Steps to Feedback (Section 7.1) for more information about this.
Relational	**Relational** Your students will benefit from some thought-provoking and engaging feedback at this stage. Misunderstandings and misconceptions can be checked for through the use of high-quality questioning. And if all is OK with that, then you can challenge your students to move on to the final level of SOLO: Extended Abstract.
Extended Abstract	**Extended Abstract** Feedback at this stage would normally focus on metacognitive thinking, including how your students made progress, what they could do differently next time, when their new understanding might be useful and why they chose certain strategies and not others.

6.2.1 • Self and Peer Feedback

A theme throughout this book is that of enabling your students to give themselves and each other feedback. This section presents some examples of how the SOLO taxonomy can help your students with their reflections.

If your students are *defining* something (e.g., defining what is meant by invasion, photosynthesis, perspective, fair play and so on), then they could use this grid to give themselves or each other feedback (remembering that feedback should answer all three questions: What am I trying to achieve? How much progress have I made so far? What should I do next?).

Figure 22 is an example of how the SOLO taxonomy can be used by students to track their own learning.

▶ Figure 22: Student Feedback Grid to Use When Defining

SOLO Stage	SOLO Description	Example	What to Do Next
Prestructural 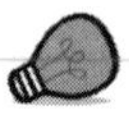	I need help to define (X)		
Unistructural 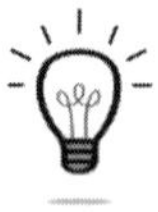	My definition has one relevant idea about (X)		
Multistructural 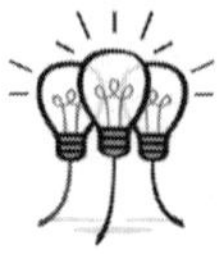	My definition has several relevant ideas about (X)		
Relational 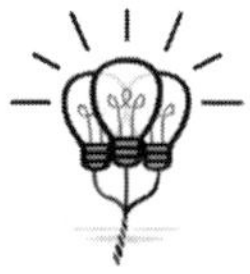	My definition has several relevant ideas about (X) and links these ideas		
Extended Abstract 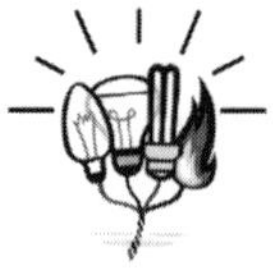	My definition has several relevant ideas about (X), links these ideas and looks at them in a new way		

When you ask your students to Compare and Contrast (see Odd One Out in *Challenging Learning Through Dialogue* [Nottingham, Nottingham & Renton, 2017] for examples) they could fill in the blanks in Figure 23.

Figure 23 is an example of how the SOLO taxonomy can be used by students when comparing and contrasting.

SOLO Stage	SOLO Description	Example	What to Do Next
Prestructural 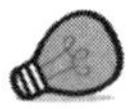	I need help to identify (X) and (Y) and I don't know how to compare them		
Unistructural 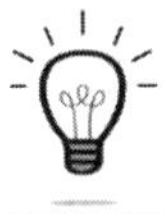	I can identify **one relevant similarity and difference** between (X) and (Y)		
Multistructural 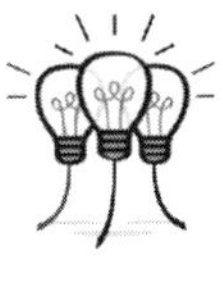	I can identify **several relevant similarities and differences** between (X) and (Y)		
Relational 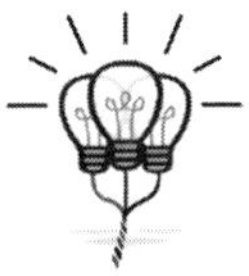	I can identify **several relevant similarities and differences** between (X) and (Y) **and give reasons why**		
Extended Abstract 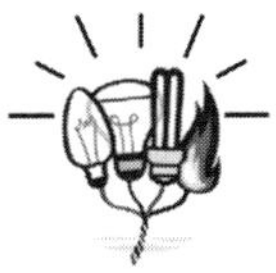	I can identify **several relevant similarities and differences** between (X) and (Y), give reasons why **and make generalization** (overall I think)		

When your students are Evaluating Claims, they could fill in the blanks in Figure 24.

Figure 24 is
an example of
how the SOLO
taxonomy
can be used
by students
when they are
learning to
evaluate claims
and arguments.

▶ Figure 24: Student Feedback Grid to Use
When Evaluating Claims

SOLO Stage	SOLO Description	Example	What to Do Next
Prestructural 	**I can make a claim** but I need help to give a relevant reason and objection		
Unistructural 	I can make a claim and **give a relevant reason and objection**		
Multistructural 	I can make a claim **and give several relevant reasons and objections**		
Relational 	I can make a claim **and explain why there are relevant reasons and objections to the claim**		
Extended Abstract 	I can make a claim **and provide evidence, judge overall support for reasons and objections and make an overall evaluation of the claim**		

6.3 • HOW THE SOLO TAXONOMY RELATES TO LEARNING

This is an
example of
how the SOLO
taxonomy
can be used
to track
the stages
of learning
in language
acquisition.

(Gordon Poad) Anybody trying to learn a new language will be able to empathize with the problems that I'm having in trying to learn Danish. I hope that in years to come I'll be able to look at that sentence, translate it into Danish and of course be able to conjugate it into the past tense. At present, unfortunately, I have a long way to go.

However, during a recent visit to Skovbyskolen, Skanderborg, Mid Jutland, in Denmark, I came across a group of Grade 9 students who were able to help me see the progress that I had made and to indicate the next steps in my language learning journey. Nothing very surprising about that, you may say, but this was a special unit in the school. It comprised students who for a variety of reasons were unable to learn effectively alongside their peers taking the mainstream routes.

At the time of visiting the school, I had lived in Denmark for around five months, and my confidence in conversing in Danish was low. However, firstly, I was determined to make a good impression on the school and know that a little Danish goes along way. Secondly, as I was visiting a special unit in a mainstream school, my expectations for the students to have the self-belief to communicate in English wasn't high. So I made up my mind: I would pluck up the courage to introduce myself in basic Danish, I prepared a few questions (parrot fashion, if I'm honest) about their learning journey, and it would be up to their teacher to translate their answers.

On entering the classroom, I was met by eight students, mostly boys whose reasons for being in the special class ranged from behavioral issues to lack of confidence or light learning disabilities. I introduced myself in my broken (very broken) Danish and asked them about how they perceived themselves as learners. Well, my fear about them not being able to communicate in English was totally unfounded. They were able to describe how they understood Learning Intentions and Success Criteria, how they were able to use a range of strategies to respond to the challenges that they had agreed on and set with their teacher and, of course, how they looked for and gave each other feedback so that they could understand if and why they had achieved the Success Criteria they had agreed on with their teacher. Of course, I was absolutely knocked out by their understanding of themselves as learners and I was anxious to find out what advice they would give me as a learner of Danish.

I asked them how I could really know if I was making progress, and all of the hands shot up with confidence. I selected Tobias to help me make sense of myself as a learner. Tobias pointed to a poster on the wall, which they had clearly made themselves, and began to explain in really rather excellent English, "Well, before you came to Denmark you had no idea of how to speak Danish. Then you learned your first words and you had one idea about speaking Danish. Now you are learning some more words, you are beginning to know more words and you have many ideas."

Signe, one of two girls in the class, built on this way of thinking. "I would say that you are somewhere between having one idea about our language and many ideas."

She stood up from her chair, walked over to the poster on the wall and in the style of a university lecturer explained, "You see, you do know some Danish words and that is great. The next step is for you to be able to really know how to put them together. After that, you'll be able to use them to make yourself better understood. You see, you'll be able to . . ."

At this point her English deserted her and she asked for a translation from her teacher.

"Ah yes, you be able to . . . apply . . . what you know and . . ."

A smile broke out across her face.

"You will be able to speak Danish!"

Now, I had a pretty good grasp of the SOLO taxonomy that was represented on the poster on the classroom wall. But of course, I was amazed that this group of learners would be so confident in being able to apply it to their understanding of the learning journey. I knew that they'd accurately described the first three stages of SOLO and were able to help me by helping my understanding in general terms where I was now and what my next learning steps should be, but I knew that there was a further step. I asked them what the fourth step could mean for me as a learner of Danish. The hands went down and the classroom fell silent. I resisted the temptation to put my question another way, and carefully the teacher translated my question into their native language.

Tentatively, Tobias raised his hand and began to explain, "Well, if you have been able to follow the first three steps, it's possible that you now know how to learn not just Danish, but any other language!"

I looked at the teacher, who of course was doing her best not to explode with pride, and thanked her and the students for reaffirming my faith that SOLO is effective in creating supporting learning.

6.3.1 • Teaching SOLO With the Help of SOLO!

(Gordon Poad) So what is the SOLO taxonomy, and in what ways can an understanding and application of it help you generate rich and practical feedback that moves learning in the right direction?

My experience tells me that most teachers have a working understanding of some kind of taxonomy, and the vast majority of them will be familiar with Bloom's taxonomy (but if you're not, then see Section 5.2). Fewer teachers I meet have a good working understanding of the SOLO taxonomy. Having said that, perhaps one of the greatest aspects of the SOLO taxonomy is that it's a delightfully simple idea that can be used by learners as young as five!

So let's begin with a question: What do you know about the SOLO taxonomy?

Let's assume you hadn't read about my experiences in the special class and had never come across any kind of taxonomy before, let alone SOLO. I realize that that is unlikely, but please humor me.

If you don't know anything at all about the SOLO taxonomy, then I could classify your understanding as Prestructural. That is assuming I wanted to use the technical language, though in truth it might be just as easy to say that you have "no idea" (at this stage) about SOLO.

If you think about it, this is where we all are when we encounter something new. And of course that includes my understanding of the Danish language when I first arrived in Denmark. But the good news is the only way is up!

OK, let's now gain some knowledge about SOLO. Let's begin with what the acronym stands for: Structure of Observed Learning Outcomes.

OK, great! You now know one thing about SOLO, and let's face it, you have made progress and your knowledge could be described as developing. You're on the way to the Unistructural stage.

Right, ready for some more information about SOLO?

John B. Biggs and Kelvin Collis first described the SOLO taxonomy in 1982. With this taxonomy, students and teachers are able to

- design Learning Intentions and learning experiences that are supported by feedback structures,

- construct and use effective Success Criteria to aid formative and summative assessment,

- provide meaningful feedback and feedforward assessment of learning outcomes,

- reflect meaningfully on what to do next to improve a child's learning and to improve the teaching process.

All in all, I think you'd agree it's a rather effective tool if it can do all of this.

If you are new to the SOLO taxonomy (and I've assumed that you are), you now have made a quantifiable step from knowing one thing to knowing, to a certain extent, many things. This is the Multistructural stage.

So are you ready for the Learning Challenge? Nearly, I would say, because the third stage of the taxonomy is about finding the relationship between these many ideas.

At the same time, you will move from surface-level knowledge to deeper learning as you progress through the Multistructural to the Relational and finally the Extended Abstract stage. These deeper levels of the taxonomy will move your thinking beyond the quantifiable stage to the qualitative category of understanding.

At the one idea and many ideas stages, we could not yet assess the quality of your thinking and understanding. We could only say how much you know rather than how well you understand it.

6.3.2 • Deepening Your Understanding of the SOLO Taxonomy

Perhaps the best way to really get to grips with the SOLO taxonomy is to use it to plan your learning about the taxonomy itself. Here is a worked example for you to complete if you'd like to:

The Big Idea: The SOLO taxonomy

Learning Intention: To understand how the SOLO taxonomy can help design valuable learning experiences for your students

Now please complete the grid shown in Figure 25.

▶ Figure 25: SOLO Planning Grid

SOLO Stage	Action	Suggestion	Your Response
Unistructural 	Identify	Identify a key feature of the SOLO taxonomy	
Multistructural 	List and describe	List and explain the key features of the SOLO taxonomy	
Relational 	Relate and explain	Explain how SOLO can be used to design progress in learning	
Extended Abstract 	Apply and create	Design a learning experience for a group of students using the SOLO taxonomy	

> Figure 25 is an example of how the SOLO taxonomy can be used to develop an understanding of the SOLO taxonomy.

(Gordon Poad) One of the big ideas I often work with is co-creation, particularly in drama. So the grid that I would prepare for my students might look something like Figure 26.

The Big Idea: Co-Creation

Learning Intention: To learn how we can use games and exercises to promote a positive environment for collaboration

Figure 26 is an example of how the SOLO taxonomy can be used by students when they are learning to collaborate together.

▶ **Figure 26: Group Feedback Grid for Students**

SOLO Stage	Action	Suggestion	Group's Response
Unistructural 	Identify	Identify a simple exercise that can be used in the rehearsal room to promote group focus	
Multistructural 	List and describe	Describe a series of games and exercises that can be used to build trust and focus in the rehearsal room	
Relational 	Relate and explain	Analyze a series of rehearsal room games and exercises, ranking them for effectiveness in developing focus, trust and collective divergent thinking	
Extended Abstract 	Apply and create	Design a workshop program for a groups of diverse performers who are meeting together for the first time to collaborate on a new project	

6.4 • THE SOLO TREEHOUSE

Figure 27 is a lovely example of how the SOLO taxonomy relates to building a treehouse, as conceived and illustrated by Dan Henderson, the graphic designer for this book.

To show how the SOLO taxonomy can be used in many different learning contexts, here it is applied to the building of a treehouse.

Prestructural

What is a treehouse?!

Unistructural

I now know what a treehouse is, but I don't know how it is made.

Multistructural

I now know that a treehouse requires wood, nails and a strong, sturdy tree. I also know that to build it will require

- careful planning,
- carpentry skills,
- the right tools, including a hammer and a saw, and
- some help from a friend.

I haven't applied all this new knowledge yet, but I feel ready to have a go.

Relational

I've marked out everything on the tree according to my plan. I understand how I will start, what I will need to do at every step and how it will all fit together. I'm now up a ladder fixing the base to the tree to make sure everything is sturdy.

Extended Abstract

I've finished my treehouse and am really proud of it. I know there are some things I could improve and realize that my plan wasn't quite perfect, but it was good enough. Now I'm drawing a plan for a little fairy house to go at the bottom of the tree. I'm also thinking of making some birdhouses to hang from the same tree. We're going to start a whole new community up there!

This chapter has covered the following main points:

1. The SOLO taxonomy describes the levels of understanding a learner goes through from (a) no idea to (b) one idea to (c) many ideas to (d) relating all the ideas together to (e) applying those ideas in different contexts and creating new hypotheses.

2. SOLO stands for Structure of Observed Learning Outcomes. John Biggs and Kevin Collis (1982) first described it in *Evaluating the Quality of Learning: The SOLO Taxonomy.*

3. When Biggs and Collis described the SOLO taxonomy, they wrote in terms of Prestructural, Unistructural, Multistructural, Relational and Extended Abstract.

4. In the Prestructural phase, students will say they have no idea or attempt the task inappropriately.

5. In the Unistructural phase, students will say they know something about the topic and be able to identify, name, remember, match or list the basic items.

6. In the Multistructural phase, students will be able to find many more ideas and describe, compare, notice patterns and find exceptions between them.

7. In the Relational phase, students will be able to connect their ideas together and explain the cause, effect and significance.

8. In the Extended Abstract phase, students will be able to apply their understanding to new and different contexts as well as generalize, hypothesize, prioritize, design, create, evaluate and perform.

9. The SOLO taxonomy helps you match learning experiences and feedback to your students' current level of understanding.

10. We have provided some new illustrations and planning grids that you are welcome to use with your students.

6.6 • NEXT STEPS

Here are some suggestions to help you with your reflections on feedback:

1. Think about a group of students you have taught recently, and identify which stage of understanding they were at according to the SOLO taxonomy.

2. Plan a series of lessons that will help groups of students move through the levels of understanding from surface-level knowledge through to extended abstract thinking.

3. Use one or more of the student feedback grids in this chapter's figures with your students to help them understand the SOLO taxonomy.

4. Relate Gordon's example of learning Danish (Section 6.3) and the example of building a treehouse (Section 6.4) to one of your own learning experiences.

5. Talk about these experiences with your students, and ask them to map stories of their own onto the SOLO taxonomy.

> "We only think when confronted with a problem."
>
> (Dewey, 1916)

SEVEN STEPS TO FEEDBACK

7.0 • BACKGROUND

Please consider the previous six chapters as the warm-up to this chapter. Indeed, everything that has gone before in this book has prepared the ground and given the justification for the Seven Steps to Feedback.

But before we start, here's a just one more justification: In Section 1.0, we began with this quote from Hattie, Biggs and Purdie (1996):

> At least 12 previous meta-analyses have included specific information on feedback in classrooms. These meta-analyses included 196 studies and 6,972 effect sizes. The average effect was 0.79 (twice the average effect). To place this average of 0.79 into perspective, it fell in the top 5 to 10 highest influences on achievement. . . . Clearly, feedback can be powerful.

Just look at that: feedback can double the rate of learning! Now that's impressive. And that was published way back in 1982. So it's hardly breaking news!

However, what has puzzled us for years is this:

> **If feedback can double the amount of progress students make, and if all teachers are already giving feedback (have you ever heard of teachers who don't?), then why isn't every student making double the rate of progress because of it?**

This is the most important chapter in the book. It shows exactly how to make feedback work brilliantly.

Either the research is wrong or teachers aren't really using feedback. Or, more likely, it is because we're not quite using feedback as effectively as we could.

That was what prompted this book and what has led to the development of the Seven Steps to Feedback. If you follow these seven steps, then you will see an improvement in the rate of progress your students make as a result of feedback. Even if they are already making very good progress, these steps will help them learn even more.

7.1 • USING THE SEVEN STEPS TO FEEDBACK

Here are the Seven Steps to Feedback:

0. Create the Culture

1. Agree on Learning Goals

2. Draft

3. Self/Peer Review

4. Edit

5. Teacher Feedback

6. Complete

7. Grade*

OK, so there are actually eight steps, *but* you will notice we have starred the last one. That is because it is not strictly necessary. We will explore the reasons for this soon.

The first one is labeled as Step 0 because it isn't really part of the Seven Steps! However, it is *very* important because without the right culture in place, the Seven Steps to Feedback will have only limited success. So it needs to be in there but as a precursor to the Seven Steps.

So in actual fact, there are Six Steps to Feedback plus one prelude and one optional addendum. A bit of a mouthful, isn't it? Let's just stick with the Seven Steps to Feedback (Nottingham, 2016).

Here, then, are the steps . . .

Step 0: Create the Culture

Before beginning the Seven Steps to Feedback, you will need to build a culture of trust, engagement and support. Without these conditions, feedback is likely to be rejected, avoided, resented or responded to under duress. That said, high-quality feedback will itself contribute to the creation of such conditions. So in many ways, the culture will influence the feedback and feedback will influence the culture.

> Creating the right culture for learning is not one of the seven steps, but it *is* a necessary condition for success.

Create a culture that says:

- **We often make mistakes.**

- **We believe mistakes are a normal part of learning.**

- **We don't have all the answers.**

- **We look to others for support and guidance.**

- **We welcome feedback as part of our learning journey.**

- **We examine our mistakes as a way to learn most from them.**

- **We are always trying to improve the way in which we give, receive and act on feedback.**

Also, make sure you remind everyone responsible for giving feedback:

1. Feedback is most welcome when it is learning-oriented rather than performance-oriented.

2. Feedback is much more effective when it is regular, cumulative and developmental rather than random and unconnected.

3. People respond best to feedback when it is personalized, well timed and constructive.

4. We should all be seen to positively welcome and act on feedback. "Walking the talk" is crucial for the credibility of feedback.

5. Convincing your students that "easy is boring" and "challenging is interesting" helps them be more open to feedback.

6. Students are more likely to seek out and welcome feedback when they are engaged in tasks that lead to a *eureka* moment (see Section 8.0).

7. Feedback should be a constructive conversation about a student's progress toward an agreed-upon goal. It should never be given—or perceived—as personal criticism.

Remember that feedback is influenced by the prevailing learning culture and not just by the relationship between the individuals giving and receiving the feedback. So pay close attention to the learning culture, and ensure you do all you can to build and share the positive aspects of that culture.

Step 1: Agree on Learning Goals

Start the Seven Steps to Feedback by agreeing on the learning goals (Learning Intentions and Success Criteria). If your students don't understand their learning goals, then feedback is not going to work well. So do all you can to get this part right! That's why Chapters 4 and 5 are the longest in this book. They are there to give you inspiration and guidance in creating inspirational and appropriate Learning Intentions and Success Criteria.

Look back at the "draw a house" exercise in Section 4.0. If you followed that through from start to finish, then you will have noticed just how much better your feedback could have been if you'd known the Success Criteria beforehand. Similarly, with the stories about Rocky Owen (Section 4.0.6) and Frank Egan (Section 4.0.7), we showed you how important an understanding of the learning goals is for your students' chances of making progress. We also emphasized in Section 4.0.5 how the setting of learning goals does not need to inhibit creativity, just as long as you introduce them skillfully.

> The Seven Steps to Feedback should always begin with agreeing on the learning goals. Without this agreement, feedback is unlikely to work well.

To add to all this, we would go as far as to say that if your students don't understand their learning goals, then you should not rely on feedback being of much use! As discussed in Chapter 6, about the SOLO taxonomy, if students are at the "no idea" or "basic ideas" stage of learning, then feedback will be relatively meaningless. You should definitely use encouragement, praise and refocusing techniques but not feedback; it is unlikely to be effective.

Figure 28 is another example of a set of learning goals. It shows a set of Success Criteria that will help fourteen-year-olds develop an understanding of Pythagoras's theorem.

▶ Figure 28: Pythagoras Success Criteria

Skill	Not Shown	Sometimes Shown	Mostly Shown	Always Shown
Recall the formula				☺
Label the triangle's sides				☺
Find the hypotenuse				☺
Rearrange the formula to find a shorter side				☺
Solve compound shapes using diagrams		☺		
Answer worded questions (in a sentence)	☹			
Rounding off			☺	
Quality of working out			☺	
Extension questions		☺		

> Figure 28 is an example of the sort of learning goals that might be agreed upon on at the beginning of a math lesson.

There are many nice aspects of this self-assessment sheet. Firstly, the Success Criteria in the left-hand column leave students in no doubt as to what they should be aiming to achieve.

Secondly, moving the faces from the left-hand columns to the furthest right-hand column will give a sense of progress. A snapshot such as this will also indicate, at a glance, how a student is getting along and what the next steps should be.

Thirdly, and perhaps most importantly, this prompt sheet will help students answer the key stages associated with the three feedback questions:

1. Understanding the goal or Learning Intention

2. Knowing where they are in relation to the goal

3. Realizing what they need to do to bridge the gap between their current position and their learning goal

Other examples of learning goals might include the following:

For younger children: When painting a picture, focus on three things: (1) use the whole page, (2) use at least three colors and (3) experiment with mixing different colors together to see what new shades can be created.

Or in swimming: As you practice your freestyle, there are two key things I want you to concentrate on: make sure your elbow is the first part of your arm to exit the water (not your hand or shoulder), and do not over-rotate your head when turning to breathe—just turn your head enough to allow half of your mouth to breathe.

Or with group work: While working in groups, I'd like you to pause every twenty minutes to give each other feedback about giving reasons, connecting to what other people have said and showing that you are listening as others are talking.

> Here are some examples of learning goals that might be agreed at the beginning of an art lesson, swimming lesson or group activity.

Step 2: Draft

Once your students understand the learning goals (Learning Intentions) and what they should do to make progress (Success Criteria), then they ought to be ready to begin.

If their learning involves producing something (e.g., an essay or a model), then encourage them to say they are doing their "first draft" rather than their "work." Similarly, if they are performing something (e.g., a physical skill) then get them to talk in terms of their "first attempt" rather than their "doing it." The differences might seem subtle, but they can be significant.

"First draft" implies that there will be some editing to follow. It is the same with "first attempt"; there is the inference that adjustments will be made. Whereas if your students talk about "doing their work" or "doing it," then they might think that (a) if it doesn't work then they are a failure or (b) once they've done it once then there is nothing more to be done. In both these cases, learning is likely to be constrained by lack of revisions and edits.

> Students should think of their initial steps toward the learning goal as a first draft rather than as "doing their work." In this way, they are more likely to assume that edits and redrafts will follow.

Step 3: Self/Peer Review

Once your students have completed their first attempt or their first draft, then they should engage in a round of self or peer feedback.

Self and peer feedback is a vital step in helping your students grow their assessment capabilities. Resist the urge to offer your insights at this stage. Encourage, and perhaps support, but do not lead this stage of the feedback process. Let your students develop their independent learning strategies.

Remind your students that they will be able to generate useful feedback for themselves and each other if they follow these steps:

1. Look again at the Learning Intentions (LI) and Success Criteria (SC). These represent your learning goals. They help you answer the first of the three feedback questions: What are you trying to achieve?

2. Now compare your first draft against the Learning Intentions and Success Criteria. Which criteria have you met, which have you exceeded and which are you still working toward? If you are reviewing with a partner, then remember to ask them to explain the reasons for their appraisals (e.g., Why do you say I have not quite met those criteria yet? What is missing or needs changing?).

3. Based on your answers to the questions above, list the actions you could take to move closer to your learning goal. If this creates a long list of actions, then prioritize them by choosing which ones you should do first, second, third and so on.

In summary, you are seeking to answer the three feedback questions:

1. What am I trying to achieve?
2. How much progress have I made so far?
3. What should I do next?

Step 4: Edit

Based on the feedback they have given themselves or each other, your students should now edit their work (or have another go if the context is a physical activity).

This does *not* mean that they should redo the whole thing! Instead, they should make additions and corrections. This could be done with a different-colored pen if doing written work, by using Track Changes if doing something digital or by attempting the skill again if engaged in physical learning.

Exam Technique

As well as teaching your students how to give themselves and each other high-quality feedback, Steps 1 to 4 of the Seven Steps to Feedback will also help them develop good exam technique. Namely, (1) read the question carefully and make sure you know what is being asked of you, (2) write your first draft, (3) look back at the exam question and check whether you have answered all aspects of it by comparing your draft against the criteria and, (4) if needed, edit your answer before moving on to the next question.

Step 5: Teacher Feedback

Only once your students have completed Steps 1 to 4 is it time for some teacher-led (or other adult-led) feedback. Of course, you might have been giving feedback, guidance and encouragement throughout the process, but Step 5 of the Seven Steps to Feedback is the time to give your more systematic feedback.

Advice, Advice, Advice

There are many conventions popular in schools—such as "Three Stars and a Wish"—but many of these are built on the belief that students need to hear lots of positive messages for every negative comment. As we hope you will have understood from reading through this book, feedback should not be viewed in terms of being negative or positive. Of course, feedback generally *is* viewed in these terms, but that doesn't mean that it *should* be!

So long as you get the feedback culture right (see Chapter 3 as well as Section 2.3.1), such that your students view feedback as information (neither good nor bad) that can be used to make progress, then the best kind of feedback is advice and suggestions. Not a little bit of "negative stuff" mixed in with lots of positives. It should be advice, advice, advice!

Advice would include ideas about what could be changed, amended, left alone, added to or scrapped altogether. And it should always be focused on the task or the process, not on the students themselves, for example: "clarify your conclusion by shortening your sentences and making them punchier" rather than "there is some need for clarity here. I want you to try harder." For more about avoiding student-focused feedback, see Section 1.5.

Also please remember that when giving feedback, you should be less of a referee and more of a coach.

Coach, Not Referee

▶ Figure 29: Coach or Referee?

> When giving feedback, teachers should think of themselves as a coach rather than as a referee.

If we were to say that a referee adjudicates and decides whereas a coach supports, challenges, trains, stretches and instructs, then it is very obvious that our role as teachers is closer to that of a coach. Of course, sometimes we should be the referee (when proctoring exams, for example). But most of the time, we should be the coach. That is assuming we want to help our students make more progress rather than simply check what they are able to do!

Sticking with the analogy of a coach, consider the similarities between what an excellent coach might do and what you might do as a teacher.

An excellent coach would do the following:

1. Welcome their team and engage them in an enjoyable warm-up (for nonsports activities, this might be a brain teaser or stimulus for thinking).

2. Give them a clear sense of what the focus for the session is (identify the Learning Intentions).

3. Ask them for suggestions about how they will achieve the learning goal or give them a clear set of instructions (this is identifying the Success Criteria).

4. Invite a more proficient performer (perhaps from another team) to demonstrate the skill (or share examples via video).

5. Give the players time to experiment and try out the skills (first draft).

6. Circulate around the players, giving individualized attention including feedback, encouragement and additional challenges.

7. Split the players into groups and ask them to give each other feedback about how to improve the skills they are currently working on (self/peer review).

8. Give more time to practice (edit).

9. Offer expert guidance on how to improve. Those players who have met or exceeded the target would be given additional challenges or be asked to apply the skills in a game, those who are nearly there would be asked to keep working on the final bits of the skill, and those who are a long way off would be given some support so that they feel as if the session has not been entirely wasted and that they have made some progress.

10. Most training sessions would then finish off with a game in which all players would be expected to try out their new skills (reiterating context and purpose).

Compare this to an excellent referee, who would do the following:

1. Remind the players to play fair.

2. Enforce the rules of the game.

3. Act as timekeeper.

4. Punish serious offenses.

5. Keep the game flowing as much as possible.

6. Provide the appropriate authorities with a match report.

7. Ensure the safety of the players.

Of course, teaching *is* different from the world of sports. But there are many parallels. And by sharing this perhaps overworked example, we hope we've drawn attention to how much more powerful feedback can be when you think of yourself as the coach rather than the referee!

Stick to the Point

As you review your students' work, make sure you refer all feedback back to the LI and SC. Don't veer off into territory that your students have not anticipated.

For example, if the LI and SC are the same as in Section 4.4.3 (shown again below), then resist the temptation to give feedback about other criteria such as spelling, choice of nouns, style of handwriting or overall appearance of the writing. That is not to say that these aren't important—of course they are. But it can be distracting and sometimes be disheartening for your students to have done their best with one set of targets, only for you to focus on other aspects of their work.

Learning Intention

To write a mystery story that uses descriptive words to create a scary atmosphere

Success Criteria

To reach our learning goal, we will be able to:

- Set the scene in the opening paragraph.

- Build up tension/suspense.

- Use spooky adjectives and powerful verbs.

- End with a cliffhanger.

A lot of teachers we work with have a problem with this advice. They say that spelling and grammar are *always* important. And they are (to a point). But imagine if we asked a non-native English speaker to read something in English out loud and the agreed purpose was to check that they could read English. How frustrating would it be if we then commented on their accent? For example:

> Too Danish: don't pronounce *t* as a *d*. It is "computer" not "compuder." Or too British: you should say "tomaydo" not "tomarto."

Or what if a child asks a parent to help with finding out some information about the water cycle but that parent then spends the time criticizing (as it feels to the child) the child's handwriting and lack of energy (even though the homework is indeed deathly boring).

Indeed, as we have written this book, we've asked different people for different types of feedback at different times. We've shared the practical examples with teacher colleagues to ask them to check clarity and suitability for their students. We've shown the design elements to graphic designers to see if they think everything is clear and illustrative. And we've talked through the concepts with our Challenging Learning team to ensure there is no conflict of message between the workshops we deliver and the ideas we've shared in this book. Now, if any of these trusted givers of feedback had remarked on punctuation, grammar or spelling, then we would not have thanked them for it! We know all of that is important, but at the time of recording our thoughts, all we want to know is do the ideas make sense, do they flow from one to the other, are they worth sharing? Not should we be using the British or American of certain words, or should we use *e.g.* or *eg* or *for example*?!

One more example, if we haven't bored you enough already. If you look at Section 4.6, you will see another example of what we mean. In that section, there is a Criteria Diamond showing nine behaviors that collaborative groups would use when being fully functional. However, as we noted in that section, it would be very difficult for each group to focus on all nine criteria all at the same time. So our advice then was to get your students to select three criteria to focus on at any given time. And so it is now with the advice in this section: when giving feedback, stick to the point. Make sure your feedback relates to the agreed-upon Learning Intentions and Success Criteria.

Of course, if your students have met all the Success Criteria, then that is a different matter. In that instance, you would need to give feedback relating to something else. Something more challenging. But that is more about making sure targets are appropriate and individualized than it is about veering off the point.

> Teacher feedback should be related to the agreed-upon learning goals. Otherwise, what was the point of setting the learning goals in the first place?

Nota Bene

Two final points about Step 5 of the Seven Steps to Feedback:

1. Your feedback should be given before your students have finished their work (or their performance), not afterward.

2. Do *not* give a grade or a mark at this stage of the Seven Steps. If you feel the need (or perhaps because you are compelled) to give a grade, then save that until Step 7.

Step 6: Complete

Now your students should finish off their piece of work or performance. Your students will have completed their first draft, reviewed it themselves or with each other, edited it and then received brilliant advice from you. So now they are ready to make the final adjustments to the piece.

It is frankly baffling how many of us give feedback to our students *after* they've finished their work. Why would we do that? If ever there was a case of closing the stable door after the horse has bolted, then that is it.

Of course, many of us will make comments such as, "The next time you do a similar piece of work, don't forget to do x, y and z." But unless the students you teach are more motivated, organized and have better long-term memories than all the students we've ever taught, then it's difficult to imagine many of them making the best use of your feedback! Imagine, though, if we were to give feedback *before* they finished and then ask them to go ahead and complete the work. Just imagine how much more they could achieve then!

But you know what some teachers have actually asked: "Isn't it cheating to show kids how to improve their work?"

Ummm, no! That's normally what we mean by teaching!

"But won't they do better than they could otherwise?" they retort.

"Hopefully yes!" That's kind of the point about feedback: it should help people achieve more than they could otherwise! That's why it's such an effective pedagogical tool. It helps people learn. But only if they make good use of it.

> **So that's why we should all be giving feedback to our students *before* they finish their piece of work or their performance: to help them achieve more than they could do by themselves.**

Of course, you can't give feedback before they finish if your students are completing an externally assessed piece of work or a national exam. That really would be cheating. But in the other ninety-something percent of the time, when your students are learning rather than being tested, then make sure you increase the likelihood that they will learn from and apply your feedback by giving it to them before they finish. As we said before, you should be the coach, not the referee (most of the time).

A teacher's feedback should be given *before* students finish their work or performance. That way, students are much more likely to apply—and therefore learn from—their teacher's advice.

Once they receive feedback from their teachers, students should edit their work (or performance) one last time before it is graded or finalized.

Step 7: Grade (If Needed)

It is a well-rehearsed argument that grades do very little for the learning process. Indeed, as Butler as well as Black and Wiliam (see Section 1.6) have pointed out, grades often diminish the power of feedback so much that giving feedback with grades has the equivalent impact of giving no feedback at all!

> **So rule number one: keep grades and feedback separate. If you feel compelled to grade (perhaps by habit or external expectation), then make sure you give advice-driven feedback first and allow your students the opportunity to improve as a result. Only then should you grade the work; or even better, get your students to grade their own work.**

Grading *can* help your students, but only if they

- understand the criteria used to determine the grade,

- can identify the next steps they could take to improve their performance,

- understand the grading system well enough to know what level they need to be at to achieve their long-term goals (of, for example, an A grade in the end-of-year exams).

Another way to make grading more powerful is to get your students to grade their own work. Of course, many teachers will say that their students can't do this, but we hope by reading this book that you might say they can't *yet* but they *can* learn how to!

> Grading should not be thought of as part of the feedback process because of its minimal (and sometimes negative) effect on learning. But if grades are going to be given, then they should come right at the end and be kept separate from the formative feedback given at Steps 3 and 5 of the Seven Steps to Feedback.

7.2 • THE SEVEN STEPS TO FEEDBACK: SOME FINAL THOUGHTS

Some years ago, it was commonplace for leaders to visit classrooms to watch teachers *teach*. This is the wrong emphasis. Why focus on the teaching when it's the *learning* that matters most? Far too often, teaching doesn't lead to the intended learning—and sometimes even gets in the way of learning. Whereas at other times, the best learning takes place when there is no teaching!

Thankfully things have moved on since then, and now it is far more commonplace for leaders to observe learning (often asking students the three key feedback questions: What are you trying to achieve? How much progress have you made so far? What should you do next?) However, the profession doesn't seem to have moved on so quickly when it comes to feedback: many people are still looking at the feedback itself rather than the *effect* of the feedback.

> **So let's be clear: The quality of feedback should be judged not on what is transmitted but on what is received and applied.**

Just as teaching is the transmission of information and learning is the receiving and application of that information, so feedback is the transmission of information and the feedback effect is the receiving and applying of that information. Just as we moved on from judging the quality of *teaching* and started now to look more at the quality of *learning*, so we should now also be moving on from looking at the quality of *feedback* to looking at the quality of the *effect* of feedback.

Why so many schools insist on having marking policies showing how to mark and when to mark is baffling. Surely it would be better to create "learning from feedback" policies that seek to examine the *impact* of feedback on learners' progress?

If you want to do this, then you could use a coding system that makes it easy to identify what constitutes draft one, what constitutes draft two and then what are the final edits. Something as straightforward as color coding in which draft one is in black, edits that make up draft two are in red and final edits are in green would work. Or engaging the Track Changes function in electronic documents would work just as well.

The main point is that you ought to be able to see the *quality* of a student's self-assessment by looking at the edits they made as they moved from draft one to draft two. And you should be able to identify the *effect* of your feedback by examining the edits students have made between draft two and their final piece of work. By doing this, you will focus on what really matters: the impact of feedback, not the feedback itself.

This will also free you from the tyranny of having to always record your feedback. The number of teachers (ourselves included) who have spent hours and hours writing long pieces of feedback in students' books as much to impress our leaders or the students' parents as for the students' benefit is outrageous. Talk about polishing a car with no wheels: the emphasis is all wrong!

Written feedback can be very useful, of course, particularly as a record for your students to refer back to as they improve their work. But to suggest, as so many marking policies do, that feedback *has to* be written is simplistic at best and damaging at worst. As we've shown throughout this book and particularly in Sections 1.2 and 4.2.2, feedback is normally more powerful when it is generated in dialogue with your students. So if you still "have" to write feedback, then have a learning dialogue with your students and get them to record the notes straight into their book before responding to your advice. That way, you should keep most people happy while still making sure that your students benefit most from your feedback.

> Judging the quality of the feedback according to what has been given is equivalent to judging the quality of teaching rather than the quality of learning. It is much more productive (and sensible) to judge the quality of the effect of feedback!

7.3 • BUT THERE'S NO TIME!

A common refrain of teachers when they hear about the Seven Steps is that there is no time! And in some ways that's true, of course: there simply are far too many things to do in teaching and far too many pressures.

However, the Seven Steps is not about working harder; it is about working smarter! It is about teaching your students how to give themselves and each other brilliant feedback so that you become less and less needed, rather than more and more busy.

Here are some ways to achieve the smarter way of working:

1. Make assessment part of the learning journey rather than an add-on at the end. Examples in Section 4.2.7 show ways to do just that.

2. Give lots and lots of verbal feedback, and reduce the amount of written feedback you give. See Section 7.2 for an explanation of how and why. Reducing the amount of written feedback will definitely free up a lot of your time (for most teachers anyway).

7. Seven Steps to Feedback

3. Remember that the Seven Steps still involve only one round of feedback from you. So in many ways you won't be giving any more feedback than you have been doing so far.

4. Get your students to grade their work at the end. Or, if you really think they won't be able to do that independently, then get them to grade work in pairs or small groups. Again, make it part of the learning process, not a bolt-on at the end.

5. Reduce the number of times you give feedback, but increase the quality. In other words, so long as you follow the Seven Steps process, then you can afford to reduce the frequency of feedback safe in the knowledge that the effect of the feedback is likely to have increased considerably. So even with less feedback, your students will still be making more progress. Everyone's a winner!

> The Seven Steps to Feedback might take longer in the short term but in the long run will save a lot of time. Plus, the quality and effect of feedback will increase dramatically! So it is a win-win for everybody.

7.4 • REVIEW

This chapter has covered the following main points:

1. James Nottingham designed the Seven Steps to Feedback to bring together all the best research, theory and practice available right now.

2. Research from many sources, including John Hattie and Dylan Wiliam, identifies feedback as one of the most significant factors in learning, saying it often leads to a doubling of the normal rate of student progress.

3. Most teachers are already giving feedback, but most are not achieving anything like double the normal rate of student progress.

4. There must therefore be things that teachers are doing that are ineffective. Or there are effective things that teachers are not doing (yet). The Seven Steps to Feedback aim to redress the imbalance.

5. A key aspect of the Seven Steps is keeping grading separate from feedback. (In fact, don't even call grading feedback. Call it what it is: grading!)

6. Teach your students how to give themselves and each other feedback.

7. Ensure that feedback corresponds to the agreed-upon Learning Intentions and Success Criteria.

8. Give your feedback *before* your students finish their work, not *after* it.

9. Get the feedback culture right, and use the Seven Steps properly. *Then* you will see the sort of impact that Hattie, Wiliam and others are promising!

Here are some suggestions to help you with your reflections on feedback:

1. Use the Seven Steps to Feedback again and again until it becomes part of your repertoire.

2. Use the Seven Steps to Feedback again and again until your students have it under their skin and use it even when you're not there.

3. Make sure you examine how well your feedback is received, understood and applied rather than how well it is given.

4. If you find yourself spending hours writing feedback for your students, then look for ways to reduce this. Feedback does not always need to be written for it to be effective!

5. Convince your colleagues that the Seven Steps to Feedback is the way to go. It will help everyone work smarter rather than harder. And it will help your students make superb progress.

> "You provide kids with great stories and teach them how to use the tools to make their own."
>
> (Matt Groening, Emmy award-winning cartoonist and creator of *The Simpsons*)

TOOLS FOR FEEDBACK

There are many tools for feedback already being used in schools right now. So rather than explore familiar ones, here are two new ways to go. The first is based on the Learning Challenge that was first published in *Challenging Learning* (Nottingham, 2010a) and then in *Encouraging Learning* (Nottingham, 2013). Louise Brown, a former colleague of ours, created the second idea: Learning Detectives.

8.0 • USING THE LEARNING CHALLENGE TO GENERATE FEEDBACK QUESTIONS

The Learning Challenge helps teachers structure lessons and helps students challenge themselves. It has been used successfully with three- to eighteen-year-olds and is now a reference point in hundreds of classrooms around the world. It can also be used to generate high-quality feedback questions.

The Learning Challenge has four stages.

Stage 1: Concept

The Learning Challenge begins with a concept. The concept can come from the media, conversation, observations or the curriculum. So long as your students have at least some understanding of the concept, then the Learning Challenge can work. In SOLO taxonomy terms, this is the Unistructural stage (see Section 6.1).

> The Learning Challenge can be used to generate feedback at different stages of the learning process.

Stage 2: Conflict

The key to the Learning Challenge is to get your students "into the pit" by creating cognitive conflict in their minds (Edwards, 2001; Nottingham, 2010a). This deliberate creation of a dilemma is what makes the Learning Challenge such a good model for challenge and inquiry. It is also the frequent experience of cognitive conflict that helps to build a growth mindset in the minds of Learning Challenge participants (Dweck, 2006). As for the SOLO taxonomy, Stage 2 represents the Multistructural stage (see Section 6.1).

Stage 3: Construct

After a while of being in the pit, some of your students will begin to construct meaning for themselves. They will do this by identifying relationships, explaining causes and integrating ideas into a new structure. As they do this, they will experience a sense of *eureka* in which they have a new sense of clarity. This in turn puts them in an ideal position to help those students who are still confused. (See Section 3.1.4 for more about eureka moments). In SOLO taxonomy terms, this is when your students move to the Relational stage of understanding (see Section 6.1).

Stage 4: Consider

Once out of the pit, your students should be encouraged to reflect on the stages of thinking they've just been through—from a single, simplistic idea (Stage 1) to the identification of lots of sometimes conflicting ideas (Stage 2) right through to a new understanding of more complex and interrelated ideas (Stage 3). They should then look for ways to relate and apply their new understanding to different contexts. In SOLO taxonomy terms, this is the Extended Abstract stage of hypothesis, generalization and application to new contexts.

To read more about the background and application of the Learning Challenge, take a look at *The Learning Challenge* (Nottingham, 2017).

▶ **Figure 30: The Learning Challenge**

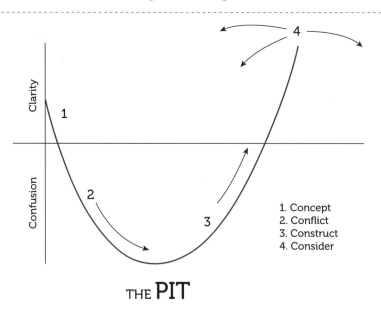

1. Concept
2. Conflict
3. Construct
4. Consider

THE **PIT**

8.1 • LEARNING CHALLENGE FEEDBACK QUESTIONS: STAGE 1

These are the sorts of questions you could ask your students at Stage 1 of the Learning Challenge:

1. Are you clear about your learning goals?
2. Are there any criteria that you don't understand?
3. Can you add any other criteria to help you in your learning journey?
4. What are the first steps you think you should take?
5. Can you think of any other ways you could begin?
6. Which learning strategies will help you make a good start?
7. Do you have any questions before you begin?

> At Stage 1 of the Learning Challenge, feedback questions should focus on how much students already know about the topic and check whether they understand the Learning Intentions and Success Criteria.

8.2 • LEARNING CHALLENGE FEEDBACK QUESTIONS: STAGE 2

Your students are now going into the pit. At this stage, it would be wise to check for misconceptions and to add further challenges as necessary. Your students should be "wobbling" at this stage but not feeling so disoriented that they want to give up.

These are the sorts of questions you could ask:

1. Is that always right?
2. What do you find puzzling?
3. Can you think of any other ideas that might help you?
4. What conflicting thoughts do you have?
5. Will it work if we do the same thing with a different example?
6. What interests you most?
7. Can you give a specific example to support your thinking?
8. Will this work in every case?
9. Can you find an exception to your argument?
10. Are your ideas still relevant to the key question?
11. What ideas are causing you the biggest dilemma? Why?
12. Is there a better way to tackle this?

> At Stage 2 of the Learning Challenge, feedback questions should open up students' minds to different possibilities.

8.3 • LEARNING CHALLENGE FEEDBACK QUESTIONS: STAGE 3

Your students should now be developing a sense of clarity, having sifted through their ideas and made connections. As they begin to come out of the pit, you can ask them some of these questions:

At Stage 3 of the Learning Challenge, feedback questions should help students make links and review their learning so far.

1. Can you develop and build on your ideas further by adding your new knowledge to them?
2. Would this always work?
3. How have you organized your ideas?
4. Which idea is the most important?
5. Can you put that more clearly?
6. How do your ideas connect together?
7. Do you think it would be better if . . . ?
8. Can you give an example of that?
9. Why have you done that and not this?
10. How do your ideas relate to your friends' ideas?
11. Can you sequence your friends' ideas and compare them with yours?
12. Which ideas are most persuasive?

8.4 • LEARNING CHALLENGE FEEDBACK QUESTIONS: STAGE 4

At Stage 4 of the Learning Challenge, feedback questions should cause students to think about how their new learning might apply to new situations.

Now that your students are out of the pit, they should take some time to reflect on their learning journey and think about how their new understanding might apply in different circumstances and in new contexts. These are the sorts of questions you might ask them to help with their reflections:

1. What was the main strategy you used to come out of the pit?
2. When could you use this again?
3. What attitudes can you identify that helped you reach this point?
4. What attitudes slowed your progress down?
5. What new knowledge have you gained?
6. What would you do differently next time?
7. How will you apply your new understanding in different lessons/contexts?
8. Can you explain how you developed your understanding?
9. Can you help others climb out of the pit?
10. How can you challenge yourself further now?
11. Can you challenge others in your group?
12. Which were the most successful strategies other people used?
13. What made them successful?
14. How could you make those strategies part of your repertoire?
15. Can you demonstrate your new understanding in a new context now?

8.5 • LEARNING DETECTIVES

Learning Detectives is an idea created by our former colleague, Louise Brown. She developed the approach as a way to help her young students learn how to give themselves and each other feedback. It has since been used right across the school age range (five through eighteen) with success.

> **Learning Detectives are students who have been nominated to stay outside of the main learning task. Their job is to look for clues of high-quality learning.**

Appointing Learning Detectives

If you are working with a relatively small group of students (e.g., fewer than twenty) then you might nominate only two or three students at a time to be Learning Detectives. Whereas if you have a large group, then you might split the students into two groups with equal numbers of them in each, with one group at any one time acting as the Learning Detectives.

Both setups involve two groups of students: students in the main group engage in the learning activity while students outside the main group act as Learning Detectives. These detectives are looking for clues of high-quality learning, for example, how well their classmates are collaborating (see Section 4.6), how well they are meeting the Success Criteria (see Chapter 4), what stages of the SOLO taxonomy individuals are at (see Chapter 6) or how much they are using positive attitudes for learning (see ASK model in Section 5.4).

Learning Detectives should prepare to give feedback to the main group about the quality of the learning that took place and the group dynamics they observed.

If you have selected just two or three Learning Detectives, then once they've finished gathering their evidence, they can rejoin the main group and engage in the main learning tasks. At this point, you could appoint two or three other students to be Learning Detectives if that suits your purpose. Either way, get all the students who have been Learning Detectives to give feedback to their classmates at some point during the learning. If possible, try to time this to fit with Step 3 or 5 of the Seven Steps to Feedback (see Chapter 7).

If on the other hand, you have split your students into two roughly equal-sized groups, then you could alternate the roles between Learning Detectives and learners periodically. For example, group A could be Learning Detectives for the first fifteen minutes while Group B is engaging in the learning tasks, and then swap over. As the groups swap roles, get the Learning Detectives to give some useful feedback at that point. This should help to improve the learning in situ rather than waiting until the end of the lesson. Doing it this way is in keeping with the routines described in the Seven Steps to Feedback.

> Learning Detectives are great for teaching students how to give each other feedback.

8.6 • EXAMPLES OF CLUES FOR LEARNING DETECTIVES TO SEARCH FOR

There are many, many clues of learning that Learning Detectives might search for.

> The feedback that students chosen as Learning Detectives can give to their classmates could be about Learning Intentions and Success Criteria or focused on the stages of learning as described by the Learning Challenge and the SOLO taxonomy.

Over the next few pages, we give examples of the sorts of guidance sheets you might offer your students. These are for inspiration only. Feel free to edit or adapt them to suit your purpose. The stylized words indicate the sorts of answers students might give.

The first sheet (Figure 31) is an example of the sort of guidance you might give Learning Detectives when you want them to observe their classmates working through Success Criteria to reach learning goals.

The second sheet (Figure 32) will help Learning Detectives think about the levels of understanding their classmates are at, according to the SOLO taxonomy (see Chapter 6 for an in-depth discussion of SOLO).

The third sheet (Figure 33) helps Learning Detectives look for progress within Success Criteria. The fourth sheet (Figure 34) focuses on the types of thinking students might engage in during group discussions. The fifth sheet (Figure 35) looks at how students might collaborate. The last set of examples shows the sorts of things that Louise designed for her original Learning Detectives, all of whom were just five years old.

Remember that in each example, where there is stylized writing it indicates the sort of answers a student might give.

Blank versions of each sheet are available to download from www.challenginglearning.com.

▶ Figure 31: **Learning Detectives Evidence Sheet, Sample 1**

Looking for Progress Toward Learning Goals		
Name: Trent Burns	**Date:** 1/4/17 **Time:** 10–10:40	**Topic:** Liquids and Solids
		Clues Detected
Learning Intention	To sort between solids and liquids and to point out examples of liquids that are not water	Astrid and Sophie reached the first part of the learning goal but didn't get onto finding liquids that aren't water.
Success Criteria	Correctly sort materials as liquid or solid using a Venn diagram (wood, iron, shampoo, shaving foam, etc.).	Venn diagram drawn and objects placed. Not sure if shampoo is in the right place, though.
	Describe *similarities* between solids and liquids (e.g., solids and liquids can be measured).	Sophie said liquids and solids can be used to make things and can be measured. Astrid said the same plus they could both be split into parts.
	Describe *differences* between solids and liquids (e.g., you can pour liquids but not solids).	Astrid said solids are hard and can be bitten; liquids are soft and can't be bitten. (??) Sophie said liquids can be poured, measured using millilitres and boiled; solids can't be poured, would be measured in milligrams and can only be melted, not boiled.
	Classify items such as sponge, rice and sand.	Neither of them made a start on this while I was a Learning Detective.
Who I observed	Astrid and Sophie	**Feedback**
My advice to them		Check whether it's right to say, "liquids can't be bitten." Also, think about all the different units that can be used for measuring (not just mm & mg).
My own learning		It got me thinking about "biting" liquids. If I put liquid in my mouth, I could make a chewing action, but is that "chewing"?
Conclusion		I think the girls did very well. I liked how they worked by themselves to start then helped each other with their Venn diagrams. They could probably have worked a bit quicker, though, as they only had ten minutes left to classify the other items.

▶ Figure 32: Learning Detectives Evidence Sheet, Sample 2

Observing Levels of Understanding Using the SOLO Taxonomy		
Learning Detective: Arwin Jones	**Date:** 7/5/17 **Time:** 11–12	**Topic:** Water Cycle
SOLO Level	**SOLO Description**	**Clues Observed**
No reasons	*Can make a claim* but can't identify a reason	Torben said the water cycle makes it rain. Sophie said rain comes from clouds. Henriette said rivers always flow into the sea. None of them gave reasons in first five minutes.
Basic reasons	Can make a claim and *give a relevant reason*	Lucas said clouds are made of water because of evaporation from lakes and seas. Magnus added to what Henriette said by explaining that water always flows downward from mountains to seas.
Many reasons	Can make a claim *and give several relevant reasons*	Lucas then gave more reasons about clouds—that they come from evaporated water that has cooled and condensed. And that the water has come not just from lakes and seas but also from plants, humans and rivers. Lucas knows a lot!
Links between reasons	Can make a claim *and explain why reasons are relevant*	Sofie said the point that Lucas made about water coming from lots of sources is an important one because of how humans are interfering with it all—deforestation, global warming, etc. I'm not sure what she means so will ask her afterward.
Applying and evaluating	Can make a claim *and provide evidence for reasons, and make an overall evaluation of the claim*	No one moved to this stage during the lesson.

8.6.3 • Learning Detectives Observing Progress Within SC

▶ Figure 33: Learning Detectives Evidence Sheet, Sample 3

Looking for Progress Within Success Criteria		
Name: Gary Potter	**Date:** 7/9/17 **Time:** 10–10:40	**Topic:** Pythagorean Theorem
Students Observed: BM, MR, MS, RK, SB		

Success Criteria	Not shown	Sometimes shown	Mostly shown	Always shown
Recall the formula			MR	SB, BM, MS, RK
Label the triangle's sides			MS, RK	SB, BM, MR
Find the hypotenuse	MR	RK	MS	SB, BM
Rearrange the formula to find a shorter side	MR	RK	SB, BM, MS	
Solve compound shapes using diagrams	MR, RK	MS	SB, BM	
Answer worded questions (in a sentence)		SB, BM, MS		
Rounding off			SB	BM, MS
Quality of working out				
Extension questions				

▶ Figure 34: Learning Detectives Evidence Sheet, Sample 4

Looking for Types of Thinking

Name: Vijay Singh		Date: 2/10/17 Time: 1-1:30		Circle the types of thinking used by the group you are observing		
Analyzing	Applying	Creating	Evaluating	Reasoning	Remembering	Understanding
Analyze	Apply	Arrange	Assess	Choose	Identify	Accept
Breakdown	Change	Assemble	Calculate	Connect	Label	Appreciate
Categorize	Construct	Combine	Conclude	Decide	List	Comprehend
(Classify)	Demonstrate	Compose	Criticize	Deduce	Match	Describe
Compare	Dramatize	Create	Critique	Determine	Memorize	Discuss
Contrast	Employ	Design	Defend	Generalize	(Name)	Distinguish
Deconstruct	Extend	Devise	Discriminate	Give reasons	Order	Explain
Draw	Illustrate	(Elaborate)	Estimate	Hypothesize	Outline	Give examples
Examine	Interpret	Formulate	Evaluate	Prove	Recall	Infer
Experiment	Manipulate	Generate	Exemplify	Question	Recognize	Locate
Predict	Operate	Modify	Judge	Rationalize	Recollect	Paraphrase
Represent	Organize	Prepare	Justify	Show cause	Remember	Rewrite
Resolve	Practice	Rearrange	Rate	Solve	Repeat	Review
Sequence	Produce	Reconstruct	Summarize	Suppose	Reproduce	(Show)
Subdivide	Use	Relate	Support	Test	Select	Show how
Rank	(Write)	Reorganize	Value	Verify	State	Translate

8.6.5 • Learning Detectives Observing Group Work and Collaboration

▶ Figure 35: Learning Detectives Evidence Sheet, Sample 5

Listening and Responding to Each Other

Scale:	0 = hardly ever	1 = some/ sometimes	2 = most/most of the time	3 = almost all the time

1. Did people encourage each other to speak (e.g., by smiling, taking turns)?	(altruism)	0	1	2	3
2. Did people focus their attention on the speaker?	(attentiveness)	0	1	2	3
3. Did people avoid interrupting or rushing the speaker?	(patience)	0	1	2	3
4. Did people stick to the question?	(tenacity)	0	1	2	3
5. Did people keep their speeches brief?	(concision)	0	1	2	3
6. Did people stick to their own convictions?	(courage)	0	1	2	3
7. Did people show a willingness to change their minds?	(openness)	0	1	2	3
8. Did people listen carefully to ideas different from their own?	(tolerance)	0	1	2	3
9. Did people recall others' ideas and put their names to them?	(respect)	0	1	2	3
10. Did people try to build on others' ideas?	(constructiveness)	0	1	2	3

Questioning and Reasoning With Each Other

Scale:	0 = not observed	1 = observed at least once	2 = observed now and then	3 = observed often

11. Did people ask open and inviting questions?	(curiosity)	0	1	2	3
12. Did people ask for clarification/definition of meaning?	(precision)	0	1	2	3
13. Did people question assumptions or conclusions?	(skepticism)	0	1	2	3
14. Did people ask for examples or evidence?	(doubt)	0	1	2	3
15. Did people ask for reasons or criteria?	(rationality)	0	1	2	3
16. Did people give examples or counter-examples?	(realism)	0	1	2	3

(Continued)

(Continued)

17. Did people give reasons or justifications?	(reasonableness)	0	1	2	3
18. Did people offer or explore alternative viewpoints?	(creativity)	0	1	2	3
19. Did people make connections or analogies?	(connectivity)	0	1	2	3
20. Did people make distinctions?	(perceptiveness)	0	1	2	3

8.6.6 • Learning Detectives: Examples From Five-Year-Olds

Figures 36 through 38 show examples of the original Learning Detective sheets that Louise used with her class of five-year-olds. As you will notice, they focused on learning behaviors. The adult writing on each page reflects notes taken by Louise as she interviewed each of the Learning Detectives about their findings.

▶ **Figure 36: Learning Detectives for Five-Year-Olds, Example A**

▶ Figure 37: Learning Detectives for Five-Year-Olds,
   Example B

▶ Figure 38: Learning Detectives for Five-Year-Olds,
   Example C

8.7 • REVIEW

In this chapter we have shared examples of feedback tools. The main points have included:

1. The Learning Challenge was designed as a way for teachers to structure lessons and for students to challenge themselves. It is also an excellent tool for organizing feedback questions.

2. Stage 1 of the Learning Challenge begins with a concept. In terms of the feedback process, this is where you would identify the Learning Intentions and Success Criteria.

3. Stage 2 of the Learning Challenge is about getting your students "into the pit" by creating cognitive conflict in their minds. In terms of the feedback process, this is where your students are gathering lots of ideas together and trying to organize them so as to decide what learning steps to take next.

4. Stage 3 of the Learning Challenge is when your students come out of the pit by constructing meaning for themselves. In terms of the feedback process, this is when your students should be thinking about how much progress they've made, what they've learned so far and what they could do to finish off.

5. Stage 4 of the Learning Challenge is when your students are out of the pit and considering how to apply their new understanding. In terms of the feedback process, this is the extended abstract stage of hypothesis, generalization and application to new contexts.

6. A lovely idea is Learning Detectives, an approach to teaching students how to give feedback originally created by our former colleague Louise Brown.

7. Learning Detectives are students who have been nominated to stay outside of the main learning task. Their job is to look for clues of high-quality learning.

8. Learning Detectives can look for all sorts of clues of learning. Included in the chapter are examples of detective work about Learning Intentions and Success Criteria, levels of understanding as described by the SOLO taxonomy, progress within Success Criteria and types of thinking that might be used during the learning process.

8.8 • NEXT STEPS AND FURTHER READING

Here are some suggestions for what you could do next so that you get the most out of this chapter:

1. Experiment with the Learning Challenge model to help you generate some appropriate questions at each stage of the feedback process.

2. Read more about the Learning Challenge in *Challenging Learning* (Nottingham, 2016).

3. Try out a Learning Detectives session with your students, and then reflect on the relative success of the approach (reflect with your students for the greatest impact).

4. Agree on a different set of clues for each Learning Detective, and then get them to share their findings with each other.

5. Read the chapter on Dialogue Detectives in *Challenging Learning Through Dialogue* (Nottingham, Nottingham & Renton, 2017).

REPERTOIRE AND JUDGMENT NOTES

Chapter 1: Setting the Scene

REPERTOIRE AND JUDGMENT NOTES

Chapter 2: Current Reality

Chapter 3: Creating a Culture for Feedback

REPERTOIRE AND JUDGMENT NOTES

Chapter 4: Goals Before Feedback

REPERTOIRE AND JUDGMENT NOTES

Chapter 5: Taxonomies to Support Goal Setting

REPERTOIRE AND JUDGMENT NOTES

Chapter 6: Feedback and the SOLO Taxonomy

Challenging LEARNING

REPERTOIRE AND JUDGMENT NOTES

Chapter 7: Seven Steps to Feedback

REPERTOIRE AND JUDGMENT NOTES

Chapter 8: Tools for Feedback

REFERENCES

Beck, A. E. (1994). On universities, J. Tuzo Wilson Medal acceptance speech. *Elements: Newsletter of the Canadian Geophysical Union, 12,* 7–9.

Biggs, J., & Collis, K. (1982). *Evaluating the quality of learning: The SOLO taxonomy (structure of the observed learning outcome).* New York, NY: Academic Press.

Binet, A. (1909). *Les idées modernes sur les enfants.* Paris, France: E. Flammarion.

Black, P., Harrison, C., Lee, C., Marshall, B., & Wiliam, D. (1990). Working inside the black box: Assessment for learning in the classroom. *Phi Delta Kappan, 86,* 8–21.

Black, P., & Wiliam, D. (1990). *Inside the black box.* London, UK: GL Assessment.

Black, P., & Wiliam, D. (1998). *Inside the black box: Raising standards through classroom assessment.* London, UK: King's College London.

Black, P., & Wiliam, D. (2002). *Inside the black box* (Updated ed.). London, UK: GL Assessment.

Bloom, B., Englehart, M., Furst, E., Hill, W., & Krathwohl, D. (1956). *Taxonomy of educational objectives: The classification of educational goals. Handbook I: Cognitive domain.* White Plains, NY: Longman.

Burke, D. (2009). Strategies for using feedback students bring to higher education. *Assessment & Evaluation in Higher Education, 34*(1), 41–50.

Burnett, P. C. (2002). Teacher praise and feedback and students' perceptions of the classroom environment. *Educational Psychology, 22*(1), 1–16.

Butler, R. (1997). Task-involving and ego-involving properties of evaluation: Effects of different psychology feedback conditions on motivational perceptions, interest and performance. *Journal of Educational Psychology, 79,* 474–482.

Carless, D. (2006). Differing perceptions in the feedback process. *Studies in Higher Education, 31,* 219–233.

Casey, B. J., Somerville, L. H., Gotlib, I. H., Ayduk, O., Franklin, N. T., Askren, M. K., . . . Shoda, Y. (2011). Behavioral and neural correlates of delay of gratification 40 years later. *Proceedings of the National Academy of Sciences, 108*(36), 14998–15003.

Clarke, S. (2005). *Formative assessment in action: Weaving the elements together.* London, UK: Hodder Murray.

Claxton, G. (2002). *Building learning power.* Bristol, UK: TLO.

Costa, A. (2000). *Habits of mind.* Alexandria, VA: Association for Supervision and Curriculum Development.

De Bono, E. (2006). *De Bono's thinking course: Powerful tools to transform your thinking.* London, UK: BBC Active.

Deci, E. L., Koestner, R., & Ryan, M. R. (1999). A meta-analytical review of experiments examining the effects of extrinsic rewards on intrinsic motivation. *Psychological Bulletin, 125,* 627–668.

Dewey, J. (2011). *Democracy and education.* Simon & Brown. (Original work published 1916)

Duncan, N. (2007). Feed-forward: Improving students' use of tutor comments *Assessment & Evaluation in Higher Education, 32,* 271–283.

Dweck, C. S. (2006). *Mindset.* New York, NY: Random House.

Dylan, W. (2011). *Embedded formative assessment*. Bloomington, IN: Solution Tree Press.

Edwards, J. (2001). Learning and thinking in the workplace. In A. L. Costa (Ed.), *Developing minds* (pp. 23–28). Alexandria, VA: ASCD.

Goethals, G. R., Messick, D. M., & Allison, S. T. (1991). The uniqueness bias: Studies of constructive social comparison. In J. Suls & T. A. Wills (Ed.), *Social comparison: Contemporary theory and research* (pp. 146–176). Hillsdale, NJ: Lawrence Erlbaum.

Hattie, J. (2009). *Visible learning: A synthesis of over 800 meta-analyses relating to achievement*. Abingdon, UK: Routledge.

Hattie, J. (2011). *Visible learning for teachers*. Abingdon, UK: Routledge.

Hattie, J., Biggs, J., & Purdie, N. (1996). Effects of learning skills interventions on student learning, *Review of Educational Research, 66*(2), 99–136.

Hattie, J., & Jaeger, R. (1998). Assessment and classroom learning: A deductive approach. *Assessment in Education, 5*, 111–122.

Hattie, J., & Timperley, H. (2007). The power of feedback. *American Educational Research Journal, 77*(1), 83.

Higgins, R. (2000). *"Be more critical!" Rethinking assessment feedback*. Paper presented at the British Educational Research Association Conference, Cardiff, Wales. Retrieved from http://www.leeds.ac.uk/educol/documents/00001548.htm

Higgins, R., Hartley, P., & Skelton, A. (2001). Getting the message across: The problem of communicating assessment feedback. *Teaching in Higher Education, 6*(2), 269–274.

Houghtailing, A. (2013). *How I created a dollar out of thin air*. Chula Vista, CA: Houghtailing Group.

Hounsell, D. (1997). Understanding teaching and teaching for understanding. In F. Marton, D. Hounsell, & N. Entwistle (Eds.), *The experience of learning: Implications for teaching and studying in higher education* (2nd ed., pp. 238–257). Edinburgh, Scotland: Scottish Academic Press.

Hounsell, D. (2003). Student feedback, learning and development. In M. Slowey & D. Watson (Eds.), *Higher education and the lifecourse* (pp. 67–78). Maidenhead, UK: SRHE and Oxford University Press/McGraw-Hill.

Kluger, A. N., & DeNisi, A. (1996). The effects of feedback interventions on performance: A historical review, a meta-analysis and a preliminary feedback intervention theory. *Psychological Bulletin, 119*(2), 254–284.

Lipman, M., & Sharp, A. M. (1986). *Wondering at the world: An instruction manual to accompany Kio and Gus*. Lanham, MD: University Press of America.

Lysakowski, R. S., & Walberg, H. J. (1982). Instructional effects of cues, participation and corrective feedback: A quantitative synthesis. *American Educational Research Journal, 19*, 559–578.

Marzano, R. J. (2007). *The art and science of teaching*. Alexandria, VA: Association for Supervision and Curriculum Development.

Meyer, W.-U. (1982). Indirect communication about perceived ability estimates. *Journal of Educational Psychology, 74*, 888–897.

Nottingham J. A. (2010a). *Challenging learning*. Berwick Upon Tweed: JN.

Nottingham J. A. (2010b). *Teaching target model: Challenging learning*. Berwick Upon Tweed: JN.

Nottingham J. A. (2013). *Encouraging learning*. Abingdon, UK: Routledge.

Nottingham, J. (2016). *Challenging learning* (2nd ed.). Abingdon, UK: Routledge.

Nottingham, J. (2017). *The learning challenge: How to guide your students through the learning pit to achieve deeper understanding.* Thousand Oaks, CA: Corwin.

Nottingham, J. A., Nottingham, J., & Renton, T. M. (2017). *Challenging learning through dialogue.* Thousand Oaks, CA: Corwin.

Nottingham, J. A., & Renton, T. M. (in press). *Challenging learning through questioning.* Thousand Oaks, CA: Corwin.

Nuthall, G. (2007). *The hidden lives of learners.* Wellington, New Zealand: NZCER Press.

Nyquist, J. B. (2003). *The benefits of reconstruing feedback as a larger system of formative assessment: A meta-analysis* (Unpublished master's thesis). Vanderbilt University, Nashville, TN.

Organisation for Economic Co-operation and Development. (2013). *PISA In Focus.* Retrieved from http://www.oecd.org/pisa/pisaproducts/pisainfocus/pisa%20in%20 focus%20n30%20(eng)--Final.pdf

Ramsden, P. (2003). *Learning to teach in higher education.* Abingdon, UK: Routledge.

Ryan, R. M., & Deci, E. L. (2000a). Intrinsic and extrinsic motivations: Classic definitions and new directions. *Contemporary Educational Psychology, 25*(1), 54–67.

Ryan, R. M., & Deci, E. L. (2000b). Self-determination theory and the facilitation of intrinsic motivation, social development and well-being. *American Psychologist, 55,* 68–78.

Sharp, P. R. (1985). Behaviour modification in the secondary school: A survey of students' attitudes to rewards and praise. *Behavioural Approaches with Children, 9,* 109–112.

Stockton, A. (2015). *10 things you don't know about formative assessment.* Retrieved from http://www.brilliant-insane.com/2015/06/10-things-you-dont-know-about-formative-assessment.html

Sully de Luque, M. F., & Sommer, S. M. (2000). The impact of culture on feedback-seeking behavior: An integrated model and propositions. *Academy of Management Review, 25,* 829–849.

Taras, M. (2003). To feedback or not to feedback in student self-assessment. *Assessment and Evaluation in Higher Education, 28,* 549–565.

Weaver, M. R. (2006). Do students value feedback? Student perceptions of tutors' written responses. *Assessment & Evaluation in Higher Education, 31*(3), 379–394.

William, D. (2011). *Embedded formative assessment.* Bloomington, IN: Solution Tree Press.

Winne, P. H., & Butler, D. L. (1994). Student cognition in learning from teaching. In T. Husen & T. Postlewaite (Eds.), *International encyclopaedia of education* (2nd ed., pp. 5738–5745). Oxford, UK: Pergamon.

Yorke, M. (2003). Formative assessment in higher education: Moves towards theory and the enhancement of pedagogic practice. *Higher Education, 45,* 477–501.

INDEX

A SAGE Publishing Company

Helping educators make the greatest impact

CORWIN HAS ONE MISSION: to enhance education through intentional professional learning.

We build long-term relationships with our authors, educators, clients, and associations who partner with us to develop and continuously improve the best evidence-based practices that establish and support lifelong learning.

Solutions you want. Experts you trust. Results you need.

AUTHOR CONSULTING

Author Consulting

On-site professional learning with sustainable results! Let us help you design a professional learning plan to meet the unique needs of your school or district. www.corwin.com/pd

INSTITUTES

Institutes

Corwin Institutes provide collaborative learning experiences that equip your team with tools and action plans ready for immediate implementation. www.corwin.com/institutes

ECOURSES

eCourses

Practical, flexible online professional learning designed to let you go at your own pace. www.corwin.com/ecourses

READ2EARN

Read2Earn

Did you know you can earn graduate credit for reading this book? Find out how: www.corwin.com/read2earn

Contact an account manager at (800) 831-6640 or visit **www.corwin.com** for more information.